The Ultimate SEO B

To Kill A Hummingbird: home of **JRMS** (James "Radical" Mason SEO: engineered to eradicate flying algorithm changes.)

By

James L. Mason

"SEO changes often: other SEO manuals don't. The "Bible" is published in electronic format also, to enable frequent free updates. Like the Bible, it's the only manual you'll need."

TOC

Overview

"Ultimate SEO Bible" sounds extremely technical, and so it is... to an extent. It is also something far more important: your path to passive income. Like any other kind of income, 'passive' must be earned: however, it can be a one-time effort, like the gift that keeps on giving.

Whether you' re an SEO professional or new to the art of optimization, the "Bible" will work for you. Experts can skip ahead to techniques found nowhere else (I know this because I invented a few in direct response to that Hummingbird bullet.) First-timers will learn that real SEO begins with the site name... and truly never ends!

Free tools help with keeping an eye on your optimization and tweaking it when needed. I simply grew tired of constantly finding information in so many different locations, not to mention alerts when algorithms change. The "Bible" began as my own time-saving device: I have been pasting everything SEO-related for years into this document.

Links to tools, screen-caps & walk-throughs with specific steps to refresh my bad memory... old techniques that still work well, tips I fell over in tiny hidden blogs. All of it in one enormous, haphazard mess! When Google came out with Humminbird, one of my own sites lost drastic income. I realized they'd done something new, really new, but what?

Suddenly I realized what the only real change is. Then it was a question of how to get around that... which wasn't easy. Hours upon hours of testing, tweaking, testing more... and then I saw it. SO simple it's hard to believe that others haven't discovered that first technique! The first discovery made the second and third ones simple... I have a secret weapon that other SEOs don't. No, don't ask or I'd have to kill you!

If I don't kill myself first, from the massive formatting job this book entails.

Now that the Bible is complete, the path to your own passive income lays directly in front you. So, turn the page and let's begin.

Niche Sites: Better Than Ever for Passive Income

Earlier this year, Google made some serious changes to their algorithms (how they rank sites for placement on the search results page.) Before those changes, people could create useless sites with lists of 'keywords' (terms people use to search) and Google would rank such junk highly, simply because important keywords appeared so often. Now? Google is encrypting what you type in to search! No longer can SEO professionals tell exactly what term brings the most traffic: no longer can junk sites be ranked. (SEO: Search Engine Optimization, or the process of making a site rank higher on search engine results. First page is preferred: whoever looks beyond that first page of results?)

Yes, Google is forever making small adjustments. So often that the good folks at Moz have made a toy - bookmark Moz's Google Forecast page! It gives you a quick view of turbulance in Google rankings. If Google has changed their algorithms, of course rankings will change. So this experimental tool shows Google's 'weather' - the hotter it is, the more things have changed. Good to know: if you see a change over many days in the last 30, Google might be testing something new. You may want to test your own SEO and see if your rankings change.

Those of us who have always practiced 'white hat' SEO (natural use of search terms, content that is highly relevant to a site's topic) have not suffered. We've been doing this all along. Your basic 'black hat' (those who 'stuffed' pages with search terms, and other nasty practices) have seen some of their procedures shut down entirely. Others, admittedly, still work well: for the short term. Google always catches on, and the site that was SEO'd by a black hat - that site plummets down the ranks. Google thinks little of such practices and removes points from sites that condone them. Google can blacklist sites, too. Yes, they can get into Google's good graces again, but not easily.

For a month or two, pundits were declaring, "niche sites are dead! SEO is dead!" Erm, excuse me but I'm still making a nice income off mine. It slipped a tiny bit: I made a few changes and now am literally making more than I was. SEO is far from a static practice: Google makes policy changes, as do other search engines, and SEO must follow suit. The basics of SEO don't change, though. Never have and never will.

Therefore here you will learn the basics as well as advanced procedures (which will never vanish either,) and you too can build prosperous niche sites. A good niche site rarely needs new content: ergo 'passive income,' or income that comes whilst you sit and watch Survivor. Don't forget, though, you work hard first. The Bible doesn't stop at SEO for niche sites, either! It covers excellent SEO practices for all sites.

What Is A Niche Website?

Exactly what it sounds like: a site dedicated to a very, very specific topic. For example, there are countless sites on Saint Bernard dogs. Such sites cover everything from food preferences to the dog's best conformation for showing. A good niche site would be "Illnesses Specific to Saint Bernards." General Saint Bernard sites may touch on illnesses, but they won't discuss the topic in depth. People who have a sick dog require sites that give specific information about illnesses such as symptoms that match their dog's, possible diseases that result from symptoms, cures, proper food, etc. AllAboutSaintBernards.com may give a list of illnesses that Saint Bernards are susceptible to, but it also covers proper appearance, exercise needed, showing techniques and many other topics. Such sites are great for general knowledge, and there are roughly 6,250,000 of them at the time of this writing. That is a lot of competition, don't you think? If you search for "Saint Bernard illnesses," you find many general dog sites which happen to have a section on sick Saints. SaintBernardIllness.com might not be a bad idea, and possibly poodleIllness.com, boxerillness... you get the idea.

Niche sites these days are merely small web sites, consisting of 7-10 pages. In the past, niche sites required an entirely different SEO approach. Thanks to search engine changes, SEO for niche sites is now no different than any other site: all sites should optimise for long-tail keywords now.

How Do I Make Money From Web Sites?

Small sites can and do create '**passive income**' - income that comes with no effort apart from:

- building a site
- populating it with, say, 10 great articles on a specific topic (articles that are interesting, unique, and grab users' attention)
- using good SEO techniques (optimizing it for search engines so that, for instance, it appears near page 1 of Google results when people search on your topic)
- placing ads on the site

Voila: income is generated whilst you sleep! Of course adding fresh articles will always draw more people to the site, generating more income.

Authority sites generate far more income for far more effort. The income isn't exactly passive, though. You'll need at least three new articles a week, for starters... and a lot of other techniques that I'll cover.

Suppose you create your 20 small sites, and a couple of them are seeing really good traffic. Can they become authority sites? Yes indeed! Start with adding that new content: your SEO won't change in the least, though. Good SEO is good SEO, no matter the site type.

Where Do I Start?

This book will show you step-by-step how I generate a decent income from both small and authority sites. It isn't difficult, even for non-technical people as I added a last chapter dedicated to technical terminology. No matter how technically-minded you are, you'll have no trouble following these directions!

So, let's dive in. Here's a fast once-over of the chapters - you certainly don't need to read in order (if you're new to SEO, though, I'd suggest you do just that.)

- Chapter 1: Site-Building from the SEO Standpoint will bring you up to speed if you're unfamiliar with SEO and related terminology.
- You're a geek? Great! Skip ahead to Chapter 2, where I delve into On-Page SEO. Chapter 3 covers Off-Page SEO, of course.
- Chapter 4 is dedicated to the use of social media for SEO purposes: this is a vital chapter!
- You'll learn to market your sites in Chapter 5.
- There is a lot of information to take in. Chapter 6 is your 'nutshell': a workbook you'll follow from site conception to receiving checks, and the vital SEO checklist for your small sites.
- Chapter 7 provides a work-book so you can track your SEO efforts.
- Once you have a good handle on standard SEO techniques, you'll want to stretch your wings and use more complicated

techniques that really pay off well. Chapter 8 provides advanced techniques.

- Chapter 9 is a handy reference of technical terms and a list of SEO tools (both free and otherwise.)
- Feel like hunting a bird or two? Chapter 10 just might have a few rather radical techniques to combat Hummingbird: a nice way of saying blow the little devils out of the sky! NO peeking, unless you're an expert. That's why this is the last chapter. I want you to really understand the basics of SEO before you learn the (admittedly simple) techniques to defeat Hummingbird and have your (or your clients') sites highly ranked. Walk before you run, grasshopper!

Chapter 1: Site Building from the SEO Standpoint

SEO comes into play before any other steps you'll take.

What is SEO?

SEO (**S**earch **E**ngine **O**ptimization) is comprised of techniques to make a site rank highly (appear on or near the first page of) search engines. Why is that so vital? Consider your own habits whilst searching. You type in a search term and hit enter. The first page of results appear: you scan down to see if anything is what you need. If so, you click and go to that site. If not, you type in another term, don't you? Sometimes, yes, you'll go to the second or third page. Most of us never make it past that first page! If your site happens to be on page 4 or worse, you just missed out on a possible lead. Simple SEO techniques can help your site appear on that coveted first page... a "Black Hat" SEO professional has no qualms about using bad techniques (those that give the SE (Search Engine)'s false results.) Trust me here: you do NOT want a Black Hat (they can have your site appear on Google's top spots, but when the SE begins to examine your rapid rise... as I said above, it isn't pretty getting knocked of Google.) Thanks to Google's recent changes, Black Hat techniques no longer work quite as well as they did. Of course certain methods do still work... but are never a good idea. Will White Hats take longer? Yes, in two senses.

You might hire a White Hat to optimize a certain new page. They use certain techniques that I'll show you: results will be visible roughly between 3 weeks and a couple of months. But your site is legit because it has relevant information that users need. Happy Google!

You might think, oh man I'm just getting starting here, what's the worst? Pissing off Google and getting results, or have to wait a week or two?

SEO for Authority Sites

What is an 'authority' site? Easy: it has dependable content that is specialized, expert and frequently updated. Note that your small site isn't updated much, if ever: ergo 'passive income.' Authority sites, although more work, definitely pay off: they're more long term than niche sites usually are and they bring in more income.

Can your small site become an authority site? Absolutely, but you can't sit on your arse and wait for it to happen! You must post weekly at least three fresh, unique articles relevant to your topic, for starters.

I started with one niche site, then built 19 more. Once I'd learned enough about SEO techniques that the small ones were generating steady income, I played with one of them: now it's an authority site. I have had offers, good offers, to sell some of my niche sites: another benefit of small sites that don't change!

SEO for Authority sites is no different than niche sites these days. Authority sites target far more keywords than a small site and can be ranked highly for several keywords: niches target long-tail keywords (specific search terms which are obviously longer than general ones. "Saint Bernards" vs. "Saint Bernard illnesses" for example.) That's the only difference. You'll optimize both sites using the same techniques.

Some say that targeting keywords is no longer efficient: I'd beg to disagree. Users still type them in: and although it's now harder to discern which terms led users to your site, use of Google Trends (as we'll discuss) will show over a period of time how your site ranks. See the section on

Google Trends for how, if you understand all you've read until here!

SEO for Smaller Sites

Content for a niche site needs to be very specific to that niche. You could add case studies, academic knowledge, industry news... the more specific the better. Innovations are great, as are graphs and eye-catching informatics.

You'll have one primary long-tail keyword that you will ensure is in the correct places (see On-Page SEO for specifics.)

What are keywords?

A major component of SEO is the '**keyword**'. A keyword is a word or phrase that people use to find a site: they type it into a search engine. These days, one can't get information about which keywords were used to access a site, but search engines still scan for natural searches. In other words, the keywords no longer have to be exact: instead of "ActionScript coding", your content could contain "...programmed in ActionScript," "If you are coding in Flash/ActionScript." Search engines have become smarter, which makes for a far better user experience but can make SEO practices more difficult if you haven't been using relevant, specific content all along. Which of course you have, as you're following this manual!

A keyword is comprised of three parts:

- The head - the main subject of your site.
- The modifier - defines or explains the subject. Locations, brands and styles are all good modifiers.
- The tail - clarifies or adds detail to the head.

All three components are not necessary to form a keyword, of course. Most of your traffic will come from your primary keyword and variations thereof. Your primary keyword will indeed consist of all three parts described above, and will specifically regard your chosen small or Authority site. This keyword is known as **'long tail'** and is the heart of your SEO.

There are two basic types of keywords:

1. Primary - Keywords most directly related to your site. These will have higher 'competition' (meaning that more sites will optimize for these keywords) than secondary.
2. Secondary - lower competition, but highly targeted traffic.

Say your business is selling horses. The obvious keyword is 'horse' of course. (Sorry, couldn't resist!) Now, every equine business out there will also use 'horse' as a primary keyword: from barns, riding schools to tack shops. Your horses happen to be Swedish Warmbloods: ergo one of your secondary terms will be "Swedish Warmbloods." Google Adwords is great to help you find those secondary terms to boost that SEO!

Your primary keywords will be long-tailed. Again, less competition for these, but targeted, specific traffic. Just what you want.

Overview of Site Optimization

You've already taken that vital first step to properly using SEO techniques to ensure your sites are highly ranked: you own this book! Correct SEO begins before a site is born -- truly it never ends until you're tired of making money. What are the overall steps to correctly optimize a site?

- From the conceptualization stage, **list possible topics and research the best keywords** using keyword tools to see if the topics were too broad, or if chosen keywords are used by so many sites (high competition) that they're essentially useless.

- During site design and development, **avoid the use of non-SEO friendly tools** such as Flash and ensure your site layout uses your keywords (see my keyword discussion.)
- Whenever you add content, ensure that content is **relevant** to the search terms you've optimized for! Don't discuss the price of eggs in China, then insert "We love Great Dane puppies in San Francisco" in a header.
- Optimize your content with **On-Page SEO**
- Set up and utilize social media
- Check how your site is doing by using free tools such as Google Analytics, Google Webmaster Tools, and your choice of free SEO toolbars.

No matter what level of technical expertise you possess, you too can use SEO techmiques to get your sites found by large numbers of people. Now it's time to get to work! First, you'll need topics for those sites...

Use Keywords to Help Determine Topics for Your Sites

How do you decide on topics for 20 different niche sites? It isn't easy to find topics that aren't already thoroughly covered!

Writers are often told to "write what you know." I decided this was good advice for starting those niche sites: make a list of my hobbies, my interests, those of my wife and kids as well. When I had my initial list, I researched each topic and narrowed down the number by checking into:

- **Products** (if any) available for sale and discussion: products with large price tags and low sales volume
- **Affiliate programs available**? (Such as Amazon - you list their products, any time you sell something you make a percentage.)
- Are there similar sites where **income is being generated**?
- And - most importantly - can you **write fresh articles on this topic**? (You'll do research, of course - but your knowledge should be such that writing is fairly easy. There

will be a LOT of writing involved: that's the name of the game!)
- How **competitive** your selected niche really is (how many other sites are targeting your same topic)

There are several vital keyword research elements which will indicate how competitive a given niche is. Understanding these elements will put you way ahead of the game:

- **domain authority** - how well a niche will perform (or rank) in SERP (Search Engine Result Pages)
- **page authority**: same as domain, but how a particular page on the niche site ranks.
- **page rank**: Importance of a page, a numeric value that is shown by several of the tools I will list. Google's founders invented the term whilst in college.
- **domain age**: Length of time a domain (www.google.com is a domain,) has existed. The older a site is, the more trusted it is.
- **juice links**: links to your niche from highly-ranked sites. If www.weLovePoodles.com gives you a link, but so does www.NewYorkTimes.com, which one do you think is going to impress people (and search engines?) NYT, of course. Your link there is a juice link!

An easy way to find great keywords for a specific topic is Soolve's free tool. Just type in your topic, press enter, and results appear from many different search engines.

Backwards Niche Selection

- Look at existing niche sites that are being sold. Get their SEO info (via toolbars I'll discuss,) and other factors as above to see if any opportunities exist there.
- TOC: On Amazon, search for books on any topic, such as German deserts. If you see the 'Look Inside' icon, that Table of Contents can provide great topic ideas for niche sites
- Forums are divided into topics - check Jokers Updates (television, general topics such as pets & movies) for active forums. A good niche idea can be found on such forums. As

always, run your topics through the steps above to ensure that niche is viable.

You now have a list of topics and keywords for each topic. Are these the best keywords for a topic? Google's free Keyword Planner tool provides great research on keywords, including generating lists of possible keywords. This tool is so vital that I've provided the following walk-thru to get you up and going.

Walk-Thru: Using Google's Keyword Planner to Find the Best Keywords for a Site

Google's free SEO tools are invaluable and used throughout this book. If you don't have an Adwords account, sign into your Google email and then hit the AdWords home page. Fill out the information and verify your account: you're good to go.

1. Go to your AdWords account. You'll see this menu:

2. Click on "Tools and Analysis" then "Keyword Planner". Click "Search for keyword and ad group ideas" and the Keyword planner tool appears.

TIP: entering your landing page (or other page) isn't very useful, as Google examines it for keywords and locates those you already have!

What would you like to do?

▾ Search for keyword and ad group ideas

Enter one or more of the following:

Your product or service

For example, flowers or used cars

Your landing page

www.example.com/page

Your product category

Enter or select a product category

Targeting

All locations

All languages

Google

Negative keywords

Customize your search

Keyword filters

Avg. monthly searches ≥ 0

Avg. CPC ≥ $0.00

Keyword options

Hide keywords in my account

Hide keywords in my plan

Include/Exclude

Get ideas

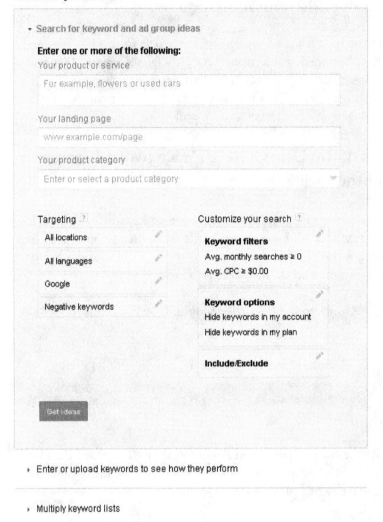

▸ Enter or upload keywords to see how they perform

▸ Multiply keyword lists

3. Select a category if you wish: it isn't necessary. If your product or site targets a specific location, by all means select it from the "all locations" drop-down. Ignore all other options.

4. For this walk-thru, one of your niche sites will be "Cat Scratch Fever" -- a site which covers cat scratching: how to stop them from destroying furniture.

   You'll type "cat scratching" into the "product or service" box. You have many other options you can and should set here, depending on your circumstances. If your site involves local products or services, you'll click "All locations" and select a single location. The keywords Google will find will be specifically related to the location you set. "Negative keywords" is self-explanatory: tell Google to avoid terms containing that word.

   SEO Tip TIP: You just might want to ensure that "Hide keywords in own account" under "Keyword Options" is ticked: otherwise Google will of course add those too!.

5. Click "Get Ideas."

   Google will provide quite a list! Some of the keywords you dreamed up may appear, as well as those Google discovers. Each keyword also has important information, from how many times that term has been searched for in a month to the Competition for a term: how many people bid on this term.

6. Here is the "Keyword Ideas" graph for 'cat scratching' :

Ad group ideas | Keyword ideas

Ad group (by relevance)	Keywords	Avg. monthly searches	Competition	Avg. CPC
Keywords like: Cat Scratc...	cat scratching post, cat scr...	37,220	High	$0.53
Pole (16)	cat scratching poles, cat s...	1,050	High	$0.46
Cat Tree (54)	cat scratching tree, cat scr...	58,780	High	$0.54
Carpet (16)	cat scratching carpet, stop...	1,150	Medium	$0.38
Pad (1)	cat scratch pad, cat scrato...	860	High	$0.50

Long Tail Pro For Keyword Research

LTP allows you to enter several keywords at once on its "Add key seedwords" page. There, you also select "exact" or "broad" matches (I suggest "exact" to begin.) The same page lets you also check "Domain availability" (URL containing any of the keywords,) "Google title competition" (number of sites that use the keyword.)

Then you can apply filters such as a range of "Average local searches" or "Average CPC" (cost per click,) "Number of words" (based on the number of words in your keyword term.) You can choose to see terms that have at least 2, 3... (any number of words) or "Has available domain."

Hit "Generate Keywords" and LongTailPro presents results as follows:

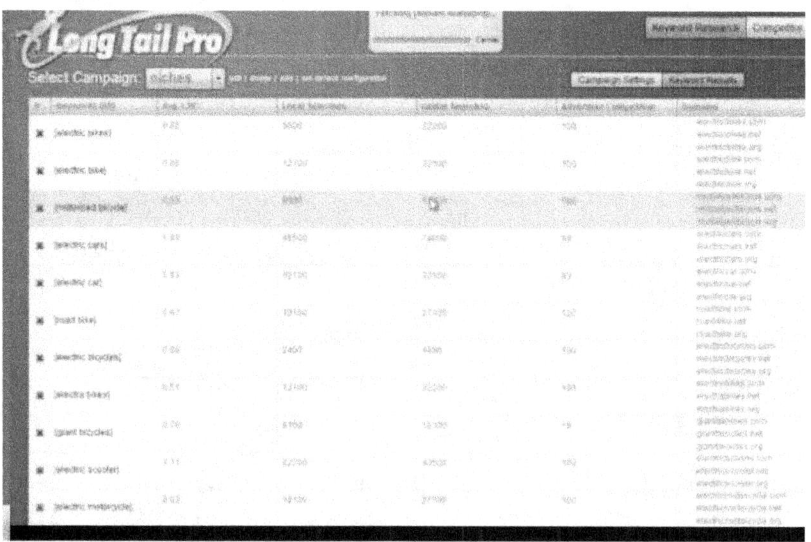

You'll see up to **8 related keywords** for each 'seed' keyword you entered, the average **cost per click** for that term (how much is paid when that term is clicked,) and even the **domain names** available for that keyword! This is an incredible time saver. Long Tail has a brief free trial.

- Analyzing results in Google

  Click on a keyword from the list (top 10 results in Google,) and you get the "Competitor Analysis" tab. Here you'll see domains that exist with that keyword, and criteria for each such as Page Authority, Juice Page Links and Page Rank. Now it's simple to analyze: you can even check if the exact keyword was mentioned in the page titles! All of this helps you figure out if you can rank for a particular keyword. For example, if there are lots of sites 8 years and older, that makes ranking a new site more difficult.

- Rank Checker

  Type in a domain and the search term(s) you want to be ranked for. Hit "Check Rank" and LTP goes to Google, Yahoo and Bing and voila! Gives you your ranking.

If you shell out for the platinum version, it adds "KC" to the Competitiveness Results: KC is calculated from all the results, including if the keyword was used in the domain/title or not, and generates a valuable number. LTP believes anything under KC 35 is worth targeting: it's as simple as that!

Still Don't Have 20 Solid Keywords? Soolve that Problem!

This is an unbelievable brain-storming tool! The following walk-through will get you on your way.

You live in Louisville, Ky. You're not close enough to any good restaurants for delivery service: not even pizza places! It's maddening, but you have an idea. What about a web site that provides links to places that deliver food 24 hours a day?

Go to the Soolve site, and type in your keyword "best country bar in Nashville" -- do NOT hit enter.

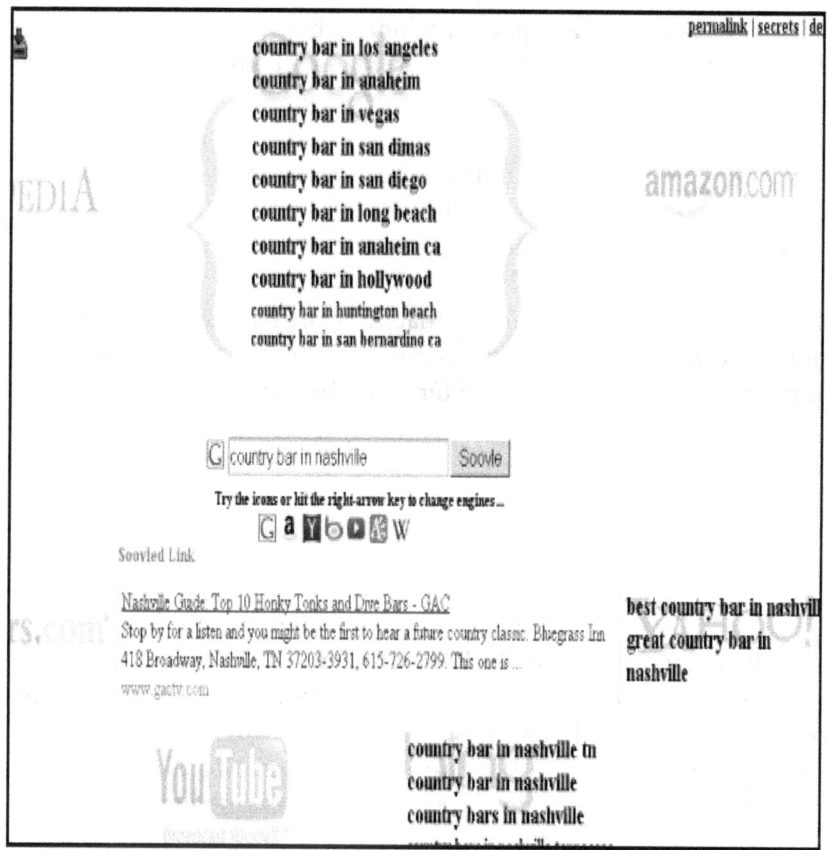

Soolve now shows results from several different sites. Simply hit your right arrow key to cycle through sites: the site at the top in curly brackets is the current one.

As you see, Bing has one keyword that looks interesting: "eat 24 hour delivery." The other sites specify cities: you're only interested in sites that provide links to 24 hour delivery all over the States - if any exist!

Grab that "eat 24 hour delivery", drag it to the book icon top left, and drop it. Presto: it's saved with any other suggested keywords. Google has "24 hour pizza delivery" -- let's grab that one as well.

Now, check out your "Saved Suggestions" box (top left.) You can print these, email them, or for major fun - click that bottom-right chart icon to be taken to Google trends for these keywords.

"24 hour delivery pizza" is a clear winner... but no real info is available. How about another keyword? "Add Term" and type in "24 hour service".

Now, change location to "United States." Look at the rise there! Click "Locations" on the left and scroll down... if you are located in a state that's bright blue, people there are using your search term quite a bit.

There are several different terms that are worth investigating. Hit that right arrow key until it's on top as it is in the above graphic. Now use your down-arrow key: each new term will be mirrored in the Soolve box.

If you hit enter, the term will display in the current app.

What About My Site Names?

Your site name will be www.**whatever.com**, **.au**, **.biz** etc. .com is, however, by far the most popular and widely-used: make an effort to come up with a domain name (site name) that ends in .com.
Also, your site name MUST include a primary 'keyword': the SEO process still ranks according to keywords in domain names!

How To Ensure No One Already Has Your Domain Registered?

I have a fun tool! Just type in the important part of a desired domain name (such as HatePickles) into the Bust A Name tool, choose whether you want it to be at the start or end of the domain and the desired length, and wow! This tool generates a list... you'll have to see to believe!

www.netsolutions.com has a widely-known 'whois' function: type in your desired domain (whatever.com) and it will not only tell you if that domain is taken or not, but suggest alternatives if so. (Caveat: if you're going Wordpress, which we do NOT suggest for hosting sites, your domain will be Wordpress.whatever.com. WordPress on your own domain is fine!)

Once you've got domains for all your sites, register them: www.godaddy.com is cheap, well-known and good.

Sites Design, Development

I suggest you stick with Wordpress for these small sites. It's simple to setup and use: you can always hire an inexpensive freelance developer at Elance to do this step for you, if need be.

You'll need to ensure any theme is SEO-friendly, of course. I have used plugins such as Yoast, as well: I'll go over these plugins and much more in the next chapter, where the heart of SEO takes place: on the page!

Selecting The Right Wordpress Theme

There are several considerations for a 'theme' (how your site will look and act.) Each of these are vital: each must be right, or people won't visit.

- **free**: no need to pay for themes with so many excellent free ones available.
- **relates to your site topic**: make sure you don't pick an art theme for a tech niche! Users will pick up on that and not like it: be gone.
- **KISS layout**: Keep it simple, stupid! (Hey, I didn't create that saying!) You only need one or two columns: so plug that in when you search.
- **Responsive layout**: this one is absolutely crucial, with 45% of users hitting the web from their phones. Your theme must look great on any device. If the design is "responsive", that means the theme 'responds' to the device it's being viewed on.
- **Social media integration**: Any theme had best provide access to the major social media platforms: FaceBook, Twitter, LinkedIn and so on.
- **Browser compatibility**: like responsive design, in that if your theme doesn't support a certain browser, you

lose everyone who uses it. How to ensure a theme works on browsers? Look for W3C standard compliancy. That simple.

- **Great navigation**: easy for users to see, understand, and reach what they've come for. Breadcrumbs are also a good idea although not vital. (You've seen sites where just above the content, there's a string of text indicating where you are such as "Home ->Animals->Penguins". Users on the "Penguin" page can click "Animals" and go up a category.
- **SEO compatible** of course! Should be compatible with the Yoast plugin.

Do not worry about colors: you can change those. The features above are vital... when you find a theme that ticks all those boxes, and preferably one that 'pops' for you, grab it! And don't forget: themes are simple to change. You are free to experiment, and by all means you should.

Finding a Developer

If you don't want to fool with setting up your own site, developers can be had on the cheap! However, you definitely need to know what you're doing when you select one. Keep in mind that if something seems too good to be true, it probably is.

I use the largest freelancer site, Elance. Developers from all over the world are available, for every conceivable price range. All you need do is place a free "brief" (or description of your needs.) You'll have many responses: there are qualities you do want and others you don't. Your best bet is to be absolutely clear on your needs in your brief.

For instance, "Need a Wordpress developer to aid in theme selection & site setup" would be a good header. In the body:

"I need a developer to help in locating and installing a good responsive theme for a new site. Developer also should be great with SEO.

You should:

= be knowledgable about themes & how they relate to topics

= Be great with SEO

= have a complete Elance profile

= Be detail-oriented

= Deliver on time.

I'm just having one site done as a test. If you work out, I'm planning a bunch more."

For the pay rate, select "Fixed" and "0 - $500" for the range. Don't get more specific.

When sorting through the results, of course you'll look at the cheaper bids first. Fine, but look at a few details before putting that developer in the "maybe" pile:

- **Number of jobs** (if you see 0 jobs, file 69 immediately!)
- **Over-all rating** (***** is best)
- **Skills**: should have "**Wordpress**" listed, "**SEO**" as well
- **Developer's location**: you don't care! It's a fallacy to believe that only American developers do good work. I've hired many developers myself: some of the best were Indians. As long as they check the above boxes and can communicate clearly with you, consider them along with everyone else. (If you are on a really tight budget, look at the Indian developers before anyone else.)

Almost done! You should have roughly 5-10 names in your "maybe" pile. Now you simply have to check details on each one. Go to their profile, and ensure that:

- Under their job list, you see Wordpress and SEO listed
- They have good feedback on jobs completed
- Look at their portfolio. Do their sites look professional? Are they mobile-friendly?

Once you've done that, you've certainly narrowed your search. Now simply pick the one who offers the best rate and time-frame: done!

Finding a Copywriter

You'll follow the same steps as you did for a developer, with a few obvious differences! Your brief will target copywriters. In the body, you'll want the same items as your developer brief with the exception of the theme-related one. Instead, you'll add:

= provide unique, quality content that is SEO-conscious

= your copy should adhere to the requested voice

(Voice: do you want business-like writing? Something more laid-back, with a shot of humor? Somewhere between the two?)

You'll check portfolios to see if they are capable of writing what you want in the style you want.

One caveat here, about writer nationality: unless you are a good enough writer yourself to be able to edit English written by a non-native, here you should stick with USA writers.

In the writing world, you get what you pay for: keep that in mind.

My First Niche Site: A How-Not-To Example!

Back when I first listened to podcasts by Pat Flynn, Chris Guthrie and Spencer Haws about niche sites, I thought the idea was great in principle but had no idea of even one topic for a niche site of my own. I had discussed it with my wife one night, asking for her opinion since as I said earlier, the best way to come up with a niche topic is to write what you know and are passionate about.

There are already tons of football-related sites: that wouldn't work. I briefly considered a beer niche site -- God knows I'm a professional there, as my beer belly will attest. My wife actually made the crack about my belly, and I promptly responded that perhaps I'd do one on how gravity works on asses after age 40! We had a good laugh: she went on to bed, and I went to the couch for some late-night TV.

After an hour I feel asleep, but woke soon enough when our overly-large cat landed on my belly. There was a documentary on TV called "Fat, Sick, and Nearly Dead." Not the jolliest thing to watch, maybe, but I was half-asleep and the damn remote had vanished.

A strange thing happened. The more I watched the thing, the more I found I could relate. Though my wife tries to cook healthy meals, more often than not I'm on the road dining on the finest of fast foods! No wonder my belly truly could no longer be called a 'beer belly': it had long since graduated to just plain fat. This documentary showed the severe effects that being fat has on your entire system. Frankly, it scared me.

As fate would have it, one of those awful long ads aired after the show. I still wasn't tired and I still couldn't find the remote, but I was certainly hunting with vigor. Meanwhile I'm hearing about a juicer, of all things. The actors raved about the effects of juicing: not just fruits but vegetables as well, your health would skyrocket, and best of all you'd lose weight. Skeptical, I whipped out my Visa and made that call anyway.

Best call I ever made. Within a matter of 2 short months I felt marvelous, I looked great because of the twenty pounds I'd shed, I was farting more than a starving man who'd broken into a canned bean factory and... suddenly I knew I had my first niche site.

I was so excited that most of what I'd learned from those podcasts flew right out of my head. I did use the Google keyword planner to check on "juicing" - it completely slipped my mind that **the domain name is not the most important** attribute. I found that thousands of people were searching for 'juicing', a nice domain name contained the term itself, and bingo! I was getting skinny, I felt great, business was going to come roaring in at such a pace that my wife would quit bitching about the farting.

My juicing niche was born.

After two weeks, I noticed it had a roaring total of 3-5 visitors a day. Where had I gone wrong?

1. I picked a niche that is **highly competitive**, (which means that many people are optimizing for it.) I had not understood the SEO principles involved: I thought that 'highly competitive' meant that people were fighting each other to get in! I learned that the only way to be successful with a highly competitive site is the reverse of niche: start an authority site. (I'll go into authority sites later. For now, simply realize that they require work, friend, and work every day. Maybe after a year you'll find yourself on the coveted Google top 10 sites listed!)

I did not understand SEO at all. Didn't think I needed to, as I had hired "experts" to build the site and create content for it. Both experts claimed SEO skills, and I had to trust them: SEO was something I had no budget for. There was **no** on or off page SEO... I knew nothing about link building. Funniest (or worse!) I found sites which offered $5 deals for "fantastic SEO tricks to bring thousands to your site," and I kept paying them to do their thing. Hey, I'd built a beautiful site with awesome content , Google will now see it and any day now I'll be top 10. Needless to say, it didn't quite happen that way!

What could I have done differently?

1. Knowing what I know now, I would never get into competitive niches at all. I could spend a day or two and find a micro niche on a competitive topic, find one that is not highly competitive. See the "Keyword Ideas" graph: high number of searches and medium competition is what really works! One long-tailed keyword that ticks both those boxes - and is available as a domain name, you're in business.

2. I'd have realized that SEO isn't simply content-related: not just a matter of keywords at all. Backlinks are an absolutely vital part of the SEO process: links TO your site from highly-authoritative sites. (I'll go into depth on backlinks: for now, imagine your traffic if you got extremely lucky, CNN reports got extremely bored and decided to do a piece on niche sites, and your site was randomly pulled from a hat. Then it appeared on CNN.com! Think a few people might visit then?) No, authority sites aren't CNN-sized: they are simply sites that are trusted to have correct knowledge on a subject. The more trusted, the better: the more authority sites that link to YOUR sites, the better. Simple as.

3. Not just backlinks, either... SEO is literally a world unto itself, one that can and has changed daily according to the whims of Google. The single most important fact about SEO is that no matter how great an SEO expert is, **you** are going to have to learn the basics and apply them. That means checking a couple of things:
    - Any changes Google has made or is considering making to their search algorithms (a good newsletter and/or good alerts help here)
    - Certain site statistics from time to time and making changes as needed.

Had I known that then, I'd have saved a lot of (useless) five dollar bills. As it is, I learned these things, often one at a time...and would apply my new knowledge then. My rank would rise a bit. Then I'd fall over another good SEO strategy, implement it... rank would rise a bit more. Rinse and repeat: now my niches sit at 3,4, or 5 on Google SERP pages and, finally, I can do what I had in mind all along.

Sit on my arse and let those niche sites do the work.

That is precisely what I did for about eight months after I'd discovered the last major SEO technique that required implementing. My rank was great: mission accomplished!

About the time that thought crosses your mind, the universe somehow takes note and gives you a good kick where the sun doesn't shine. It delivered me a really good one. Well, not exactly me, but it might as well have been me: it affected my wife deeply, and every married man out there *knows* what that means.

All his life, her father has run a small local bakery that he inherited from his father. It is a superb little bakery: they pay great attention to detail, and my father in law bakes like no one else. Unfortunately.

He had a massive stroke that paralyzed his left side and left him mostly speechless. My wife was heartbroken and terrified, for more than just the obvious reason. As her dad had been the baker (the ONLY baker) in that shop, my mother-in-law was forced to try every option possible to keep the shop going until his return (not "if," "until.") She put ads everywhere, tried out several bakers and finally, out of sheer desperation, she herselftried to bake. That bakery slid downhill faster than a racer at the Olympics. Yes, my income was sufficient, but only for my wife and myself. It would take time to put together another 20 sites... and that is when it hit me.

My father in law isn't the only person in that kind of shape or need. A lot of people have accidents and can't continue life as it was... and here I sat with this ungodly amount of SEO knowledge that I had literally garnered from all over the internet. Had I had ONE THING when I began the whole SEO process, I'd have been in the black and making a decent income witin a matter of a couple of months instead of the fifteen months that transpired.

Gee, I wonder what that one thing could be?

You're reading it, of course.

Don't think for one hot moment I didn't buy a ton of these damn books myself: of course I did (they were cheaper than the 5 buck specials!) Although some of those books had SOME knowledge, not a single one had even *half* of the SEO techniques I gathered. Why should that be so? Likely because I'm both anal and determined: I wanted my sites top 10 on Google, period. AND I wanted to be sure

I wasn't missing a technique that would either get them there or keep them there... truly I put a new meaning to research for these SEO nuggets you'll find in here.

At least that's what I told myself: that I was creating a veritable SEO Bible. In reality, I had had no intention on putting together a book: I want to write as much as my wife wants to grow a... you know. But her father in law was involved, in my mind. If he'd had this book back then, they'd not have lost their house. His insurance and savings ran out in a year: more than enough time for 20 niches and a couple of authorities to kick in. And so many other people in need... I had no choice. (And I do mean no choice: my wife has been in on the great SEO niche project from the beginning. The thought hit both of us at the same time about her dad and others like him: never put all your eggs in one basket, period. Especially when you're the one baking the bread that lines those baskets.) I may have conceived the notion that this book would help a lot of people: my wife was absolutely hell-bent.

What can you do!

Google's Latest Change (Hummingbird)

Hummingbird is deceptively simple, according to Google: keep on using solid white-hat SEO techniques and all will be well, they insisted.

Is that why one of my small sites that generates constant passive income suddenly dropped to 0 income? Of course I follow good SEO techniques: my nches generate enough passive income that I am able to live better than I normally would. Not to mention the authority sites that had grown from several of the niches. I wasn't alone: many, many businesses were bewildered at a sudden loss of unique traffic numbers. SEO experts became more valuable than gold: "fix my site, fast! No matter the cost." To really comprehend what has happened, you need to understand basic SEO as well as how Google's Hummingbird functions.

Main Concepts Behind Hummingbird

Conversational searches: Google has leapt onboard the vocal train driven by Android at the moment. If you happen to have an Android phone, you'll notice the 'hands free' option (speech to give commands, send texts, and search) works better than ever. If you have a mike on your desktop, you can use the little mike on Google's search: simply click and dictate your search. Google responds either as usual or with something brand new, an informational 'card' containing facts about the topic you searched on.

That "card" is an income killer, period. It can take up most of the room above the fold and, far worse, contain exactly what the user needed about a topic. How is that such a bad thing? Here's a fast example.

You have a site that contains all things Obama. You find the man fascinating! His life prior to his presidency, where he's lived, what neighbors have said about him: these and many more facts are on your site. The site is popular, and makes a decent income for you - until now. Now? Not a dime. What happened? To find out, you'll become Mr. Iwanna Knoe, just a student looking to do a report on Obama. Iwanna hopes his new angle on Obama will get him an A on this paper: how Obama and his brothers or sisters were raised to think about certain subjects. As he's out at the student grill, Iwanna will use his Android S4 to get him started.

Iwanna (and you) will first need to know how many sibs Obama has. Type into Google: "How many siblings does Obama have?" (Iwanna spoke to his phone: you are mimicing that conversational search.) Chrome maximized shows this result:

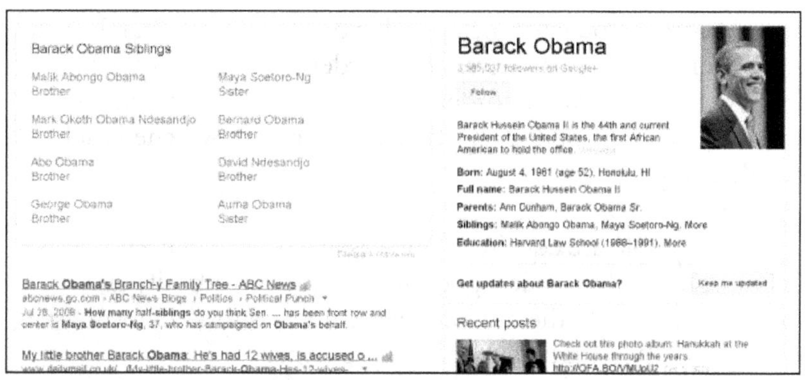

That's a different result, isn't it? THAT, my friend, is the new Google "card" or "knowledge panel." And that's the culprit behind your loss of income. Why would Iwanna (or anyone else) scroll past that card in search of more information? Iwanna has the exact information he needed: he's done. Your Obama site along with any others have lost out on Iwanna's visit. Iwanna, and countless other users who searched for that information!

And now you too see. How has Google managed to amass these details and arrange them in such a neat format?

Back in May, Google launched a beast known as "Knowledge Graph." This is really a new way to store data: instead of just facts, Google is storing concepts, or how people/places/objects relate to each other. We're not just talking about a few new concepts, either... based on 3.5 ***billion*** (and growing by the minute) facts, Google has compiled 500 million "entities" - nouns, really. When you consider all the searches that have been run on Google over the years (hello big data,) you must realize that they likely have a good idea of what users really want to know regarding a given 'entity.'

That Knowledge Panel is bad enough, but Google has another new visual result: the "knowledge carousel." As if the card isn't bad enough, the carousel provides mutliple related items. Another brief example.

In this case, you are an obssessed Monroe fan. Your site, which has been up for more than 20 years, has everything there is regarding

Marilyn Monroe. You even include a list of films which searchers can sort according to various filters: in the order Marilyn shot them, in order of popularity, even in order of the exact amount of time she was visible! You're proud of this latter: you actually watched each film with a stopwatch.

Many other people are equally as obssessed, so you have forums as well. For years you've made a good living off this authority site. While it hasn't dropped to 0, the rate of 'unique new visitors' almost has! Why? Google "What are Marilyn Monroe films?"

Meet the Google "Carousel" which not only displays those films, but even has a search similar to yours!

For SEO purposes, this is a nightmare no matter which side you are on: the SEO client or expert. Many experts are lost: how does one deal with such a plethora of information? It's impossible to optimize for, because there's no way to know what is going to trigger one of those cards. Is there?

I might have a card or two up my own sleeve, but I'd prefer that you learn SEO correctly first. Walk before you run, so to speak. (Of course if you're on the track team, just hit Chapter 10 now!) .

Chapter 2: On-Page SEO

What is "On-page SEO?" On-page SEO is optimization under your (or your webmaster's) direct control. Off-page SEO you can control to a minor extent, but as you'll see in the next chapter, Off-page SEO relies on the actions of users, visitors and even other publishers.

Content is, of course, a major on-page factor for SEO optimization. Others include certain HTML tags, correct links, keyword density and proper keyword placement. I'll go over each of these so that you have a firm understanding.

Good page content

Good content is far more than just content that contains keywords. Good content must be relevant, supply a demand, and be linkable.

Relevant Content

"**Relevant**" content means that it relates directly to the main topic. When a user types in "vampire novels", the page they land on should discuss vampire novels: perhaps list the top 10 favorites, the latest ones available, or those the page owner prefers. All of these are 'relevant' to the user's search. They also fill the user's demand: they wanted to know about such novels.

Content freshness - Good page content is fresh content that is updated frequently. For niche sites, this isn't so important. The content's relevance is, though!

Linkable Content

"Linkable" content is able to be reached via a link. The best content available is worthless if people can't access it! Examples of content that is not linkable include locked pages that require a log-in, content that can't be shared, certain slideshows and certain Flash media.

Links

SEO-Conscious Links

Wordpress gives you several options for links to your pages: the default (which ends in the page number) or the 'pretty url' which contains the category and/or the page name. You can find this under "Settings" or the Yoast plug-in, which I cover a bit further down.

Navigation links on your pages are often overlooked. Take a menu, for example: a really lovely one with graphic buttons which change colors on mouse-over. You love yours: took a while to create buttons to match your scheme.

Search engines don't read graphics! So kill the pretty buttons and go with text links.

Thanks to recent Google changes, certain types of links will get serious penalties against your site:

- **"Do-Follow"** links from guest blogs If you post guest blogs on another site and put links to your own site in that content, Google prefers that you make these links "nofollow". (This may come as a surprise, but when Google runs across a "nofollow" link, the bots won't crawl that link! Easy enough to designate a link as "nofollow":
  <a href="http://www.SneakLinkMySite.com" rel="nofollow">Some major keywords</a>
- The best SEO practice regarding do-follow and other links is, of course, to check Google's "Link Schemes" page (under

Webmaster Tools. You may need to enable Webmaster Tools from your Google account, if you haven't done so already.)

- **undisclosed sponsored posts** - These posts look like innocent responses to a blog regarding, for instance, a product the original blogger discussed. In reality, a company paid for that link. Neither Google nor the FTC are big on this practice: "Conflict of interest," as usual. Fair enough: don't accept money to place links on your niche sites.

Unacceptable Links Grow Daily.. Help!

Search for sites that discuss yours, but don't include a link to it: it happens! You have the perfect niche site on feathered fishing lures. It's mentioned on several other sites, with no link. You can politely request they add a link: this is the **natural link** Google loves. Moz to the rescue: their free Fresh Web Explorer tool will find such naked mentions. (My term, that!)

Use social media to generate natural links: never just create a profile (on LinkedIn, for example) and think you're done. Interact in their groups: answer questions about your topics. You'll naturally generate links like that.

Keyword Usage

Keyword Density

This has become more important than ever, in light of Google's latest changes. "Density" is the percentage of keywords in your content. The number of keywords per page has changed over the years. Currently, 1 is acceptable and it had best be a natural variant of the term! "Keyword Stuffing," or cramming in as many as possible, will lose points for your site. Do not do it.

Keyword Placement

There are certain very important places in your content where keywords count highly: in the title, the META description, and headers. Don't use the exact same term! Try to use any keyword 'naturally' as if you're discussing the subject with a friend. Google thinks highly of keywords used in a natural way, and those which appear as similar terms. The thesaurus is your friend.

Keyword Prominence

Keyword prominence is, almost literally, a step away from keyword placement! Your secondary keywords (or variations thereof) should be NEAR where you placed the primary. Near the title: near headers, and even within first 150 words (above the fold.)

HTML-level SEO: Game of tag, anyone?

If you've found a good SEO plugin or two, these steps will be simple: you'll just fill in the blanks and check off certain boxes! It's just as easy to do in plain HTML, although you must have a good understanding of a few HTML features first.

Briefly, HTML consists of opening and closing tags, for instance **<h1>** and **</h1>**. Just looking at these tags, it's obvious that they refer to Header 1: always remember, though, what you open you must close! In HTML, the forward slash closes tags.

Meta tags (only visible in HTML) provide a description of page contents, the title, and even a list of keywords. As you can imagine, meta tags are absolutely vital to good SEO techniques! If you're using a good SEO plug-in, the meta tags will be listed for you to simply type in the data. Otherwise, you'll click the HTML editor, scroll to the top of the page and either enter the tags yourself if they're not there or edit them.

The tags most vital for SEO purposes are:

- "**title**": the page's title. Must contain the primary keyword and contain less than 70 characters. Google uses your title in your listing, so it's vitally important to not only use the keyword, but ensure that the title grabs attention!
- meta "**description**": a description of the page's topic. Here again you'll use your primary keyword. Search engines generally truncate anything longer than 160 characters: keep that in mind when creating your description. Again, you'll want to grab attention here.
- "**ALT**" tags: these describe a picture on your page. Alt tags aren't just useful for SEO purposes: the blind literally hear the description, as they can't see the picture.

Below is the top of a typical page: there are other meta tags that can be used, but these are key. For a detailed HTML discussion which includes writing your own HTML file, see my HTML Primer.

```
<!DOCTYPE HTML PUBLIC "-//W3C//DTD HTML 4.01//EN"
"http://www.w3.org/TR/html4 /strict.dtd">
<html>
<head>
<title>Laser SEO for Niche Sites</title>
<meta name="keywords" content="SEO, SEO for niche
sites, SEO bible, SEO meta tags, SEO social media">
<meta name="description" content="Detailed steps:
how to use SEO to ensure a site ranks highly.">
</head>
<body>
<p><img src="seo-tip.jpg" width="150" height="70"
alt="SEO tip - do not use Flash" /></p>
```

Tools to check your content optimization

Yoast Plug-in

The **Yoast Wordpress plug-in** will make SEO much easier on you! It literally gives you a red, yellow or green light depending on how well you've optimized your page. If the light is red or yellow, Yoast gives recommendations on how to improve. Can't be beat, and it's free. Download it here.

All-in-One Plug-in

Once set up, add a new post - on your dashboard post-list there are 3 new columns: SEO title, SEO description, SEO keywords (for every post.) Changing an indivdual post's attributes will over-ride those you set for the site. If you let All-In-One auto-generate your titles, it will simply take the post's title. I can think of many occasions where I'd rather over-ride that.

My post title is "LA Rams' New Pics" - I edit it, and now Google will see "LA Rams' New Picks | California's Best Football News". You can see where that comes in handy! People reading the blog don't need that extra information: users viewing SERPs certainly will.

In a new post, scroll below your post editor box to see what All in One has added. Very cool. You'll see the snippet, title & description as it will display in Google. You'll see the defaults: most of the time you'll want to change those, and now it's simple. For 'description', don't forget you're only allowed 160 characters. Use your keywords and... use complete sentences.

Browser toolbars

Install the free MozBar (toolbar for Chrome or Firefox): it checks SEO content (and much more) on your own and other sites.

The free SEOQuake toolbar (Firefox, Opera and Safari) provides an enormous amount of information.

The SEO toolbar section has more information on these toolbars.

Code Optimization

Once that niche site is complete, it's time for other optimizing techniques. Content and backlinks are vital, but usability is key: if users don't find your site easy to use (for instance, if it takes quite a while to load, that's a strike against usability,) you might get traffic but you assuredly won't keep it: your bounce rate climbs.

Bounce rates rising can happen because of slow page load speeds. You want your pages to load quickly on all devices. Google Webmaster Tools has just the ticket: PageSpeed Insights. Once there, click "Other Resources" and then "PageSpeed Analysis." Type in your URL, and the tool measures load speed for both mobile and desktops. It scores from 1-100: the higher the better. 85 or above is good. It analyzes and reports on improving performance by:

- time to load above-the-fold content
- time to load full page

Of course speed can be determined by a user's connection, so this tool only measures network-independent aspects such as HTML structure, CSS, and images. It provides suggestions on how to improve page load time. Well worth a visit!

No Canonical Issue

Many links look alike, yet a web server could return different results. Google finds these on your site, backlinks, etc. These for example:

- Boogerexam.com
- www.Boogerexam.com/index.html
- www.Boogerexam.com
- Boogerexam.com/home.asp
- Boogerexam.com/index.php

Google picks the URL that seems best from the list. What if it isn't? There are ways to ensure that the proper URL is always used:

- Do not use the Google URL removal tool! Your site won't be listed for 6 months.
- Pick the one you want, use it everywhere on your site.
- 301 redirect: if someone requests an URL you don't want, they'll be redirected automatically to the correct one..

Chapter 3: Off-Page SEO

What is "Off-page SEO?" Up until 10 years ago, it was all about links to your site, those links being "off YOUR page" and on someone else's. Off-page SEO is really pure marketing. It includes:

- **backlinks**
- **social media** use (much more on that in Chapter 4) - using Facebook, Twitter, LinkedIn and other networks to get recognition
- **cross-linking** - links within your site: for instance links on one page referring to another page
- **press releases** - creating press releases which are relevant to your topic. Perhaps announcing a new site is going live, etc.
- **answering questions** (Yahoo Answers, cha-cha, Answer Bag...) Always brings good authority with it!

Several factors are involved with off-page SEO:

Links, of course (although less so than in times past: Google's Penguin and unnatural link penalties are partially to blame.) However, links that exist on authority sites are golden.

How anal does Google get about links these days? By checking such esoteric data as:

- The position of the link on the page (above or below the fold?)
- How many unique domains point to your page?
- Link diversity (text, graphics, etc)
- Authorship (links placed in content from verified, known authors.)

Backlinks

Backlinks are more important than ever for SEO purposes now that Google has essentially pulled the plug on keyword searching. What is a back-link? Exactly what it sounds like: a link somewhere else that points to your site or a page on your site. The more important the site where the backlink resides, the more points you get from Google. Why?

Google knows that if a site with enormous authority (say, Forbes.com) has an article with a link to your site in it, your site must be relevant or Forbes wouldn't have used it.

The fun part of the backlinks game is twofold:

- Finding the best locations for backlinks for your specific site
- Plunking your backlink there, without appearing "spammy" (just advertising copy, nothing of real value.)

This is, arguably, the single most important SEO effort you'll make. Ergo I'm going to walk you through the process, one step at a time.

Once your sites have been live for several weeks, use this free Moz Site Explorer tool: it will list links to your site along with the authority of each.

What Should A Backlink Point To?

Articles or blogs are usually a good bet: make sure your content is unique, very well written, and of course related to your backlink. If your article is full of excellent content, great facts and figures and is appealing to the eye, it is known as 'linkbait' because people will link to it. This gives your backlinks more weight of course!

SEO Tip TIP: watch it using keywords in that article. Google will pick up the subject from the other article text: you stuff keywords in, you'll piss off Google!

Backlinks In Articles Or Comments

Articles can be submitted to any number of places: some even pay!

Squidoo, for example. They call their articles "lens", by the way. One way to make a few bucks is to include affiliates in your article, such as Amazon products if you're an Amazon affiliate. Someone wrote an article on "Why I love My Ipad" and included several Ipad accessories for sale. They could have included links to a site they own, as well.

Ezine Articles is unpaid, but exposure is incredible. Each article is read by two humans... Ezine expects experts in whatever the topic covered. Well-written knowledge, too. (There is a 2 link maximum per article, here.)

You can't write? Elance has thousands of copywriters, some unbelievably cheap. (Beware! Three bucks for 500 words can get you dross, unreadable English, a copy of another article (!!!), or all three.) Make sure you check out everyone who replies to your (free) brief: ensure they've had clients before, and the feedback is good. When you do find a good, affordable writer -- hang on to them!

Find authority blogs that cover your topic and make comments, including a link to your site or blog every now and then. (This isn't something you want to do often, as I mentioned earlier.) How to find high-ranking places to comment? A free tool, SEOquake, provides plug-ins for Firefox, Opera, and Safari which will let you search for highly-ranked sites (and a lot more!)

Backlinks In Social Bookmarking Sites

Social bookmarking sites are good as well. Digg is very well known: there is an enormous community who reads articles submitted there, and rates each one with 'diggs'! Instead of uploading an article, on Digg you upload a link. Your article will appear alongside the likes of the New York Times, Huffington Post and more!

Reddit is a massive group of communities - sort of like gigantic forums. You actually communicate, here: which means you do not just post a link and run. Oh, you can: it will simply vanish. Better to respond to questions, engage in conversation - then drop a link where it makes sense. Check this Reddit page for details.

Social Poster allows you to put an URL, a title, description and tags - then simply click Reddit, Digg, and many more. Your link will be sent to however many places you choose.

Backlinks in an RSS Feed

RSS Feed Aggregators allow readers to get news of all their blogs/sites/other media in one place and help them find new places to follow. Not the strongest backlinks around, but when you create a new blog entry, for instance, the aggregator automatically updates. One less step for you!

For example, if you regularly submit to HubPages, your RSS feed link is under your profile. Bet you didn't know you had one, did you!

Technorati is a geek aggregator: most content is geek-related.

Netime Channel is a one-stop shop: they even tell you how to set up your own RSS feed. Of course you can submit it to them as well.

FeedAgg is one of the best: they cover everything under the sun. Adding your feed is simplicity itself: do it here.

Backlinks In Forums: Best Way To Go, But Time-Consuming!

You'll need to find forums which cover your topics, of course. The bigger the forum the better, as a rule. Again, no spamming! Forums are communities of people who hang out and talk... so busting in and dropping a link is deeply frowned upon.

Read a bit of the forum: get a feel for how people post there. Then respond to a few posts yourself: see if you can't get into a conversation. Signatures are great places for backlinks, on most forums. Always check the rules.

Example: off-track Thoroughbred hunters and jumpers niche site

You google "hunter jumper forums" and the first listing is the venerable Chronicle of The Horse forums. A quick look shows that these forums are very active, so you first read their posting rules (you'll read the rules for every forum you're considering.) All is well: get an account.

Now you'll scan through topics and questions, answer a few. No links for a bit - unless someone asks about Thoroughbred off the track hunters. There you can reply with a link but NOT if it's one of your first 10 posts.

Backlinks in Blogs

Only makes sense: do a search for blogs that relate to your topic. Read recent posts, add a comment with a link to your site - but a relevant comment. Not just words with a link to your site!

TIP: Nofollow blogs - these are blogs that mark any links as 'nofollow'. Search engines then ignore any links! Make sure if you're using the blog technique, they don't have 'nofollow' set. Unfortunately, these days many blogs will have 'nofollow' set, but it's definitely worth checking into.

The problem with setting your material as 'dofollow' is that you can invite a lot of spam. Easy solution: use the Askimet or Captcha plugins, both of which kill spam. (If your own site is "NoFollow", you won't get much traffic or comments!)

Sneaky Backlinks

1. Get your unique article posted on a site that covers your niche - many sites will accept $5 and allow one good link inside the article. This takes research on your part: using the free MozBar (toolbar for Chrome or Firefox) will simplify matters. You want a site which has a high rank, good link counts and is trusted. Search for your keywords, check the SERP and off you go.
2. Search correctly for good link pages and resources that link to topics like yours:
    - "German applesauce" + "helpful resources"
    - "German applesauce" + "links page"
    - "German applesauce" + allinurl:links
3. Broken link hunt: this one is funny but so help me it works! Find a page with a load of links to pages that cover your topic. Check for links that don't work (there are ALWAYS some that don't!) Now you simply send a note to the webmaster, informing them they have broken links and would they kindly replace them with your active one? Works like a charm!

4. Actionable link building: hold an event, start a controversial topic (present both sides.) SemRush has a thorough list of ways to build links based on value.
5. Put out a press release: www.empowerednews.net is Google-approved and only charges $2 per release (major sites such as PRWeb demand $300+, if you please.)

TIP: You don't want a bunch of links from any one method: Google frowns on that. You do want a limited number of high quality links. .

Chapter 4: SEO & Social Media

SEO isn't just linking, content, and site architecture: these days, one must actually build relationships, enhance social identity and actually engage. Social media has become key in SEO techniques. Now if you have a question about how your site is perceived, for example, you ask your followers on Twitter. Engage with them, and there's no end to the learning. Not to mention others get involved, and presto: yet another way to build targeted traffic.

Perhaps you already dabble with social media sites such as Twitter, Facebook, LinkedIn and/or major topic-specific forums such as Wilmington, Delaware real estate. Such social networks are absolutely invaluable for SEO and/or marketing purposes:

- Facebook: the #1 network for b2c AND b2b because there, you deal with your users/ get leads as well as strictly dealing with client.
- Twitter: B2C. Both networks require a lot of posting when you first begin: I learned a lot about what to post and the reverse.
- LinkedIn: Major b2b communications. Join groups relating to your business here but be careful about your content: these posts can haunt you. However, good responses up your authority and these days, more and more LinkedIn posts are linked on Google's SERP.

- Google Plus: Ever more important, this network. Make a post in a group and within seconds there's a link to it in Google search results!

I'm going into detail on each of these SM sites because it's absolutely vital that you make good use of them.

LinkedIn

LinkedIn is the largest B2B platform. It is distinctly different than any of the others, in that it is meant to be purely business-related: businessses contacting other businesses, establishing authority, branding, and much more.

Slowly, though, LinkedIn has evolved into a sort of hybrid: business-related, yes, but also social via the LinkedIn groups which have sprouted and grown so radically.

Other than your LinkedIn profile, those groups are absolutely vital to becoming an authority and establishing brands, if you so choose, for your niches. (If it sounds like I'm really discussing an authority site... I am!) However, even niches can take advantage of all that LinkedIn offers. Just a few major points:

Your profile is vital! You'll want a few personal facts: people prefer dealing with a human over a business (or a site.) However, remember where you are. No relaxed profile here! Keep it straightforward, simple, and business-like. The occasional joke is fine, but 'occasional' is key.

Every enterprise has at least one group devoted to it. You'll want to join groups for those niches that best fit the business world, or those you think could well become authority sites. Before you join, though, do your research!

If the group allows reading prior to membership, give it a good read. Are people posting mainly their own blogs, or is there good conversion there? Avoid the former: it will do you no good.

How long has the group been established? How many people are in it? Are the conversations actually relevant to the topic? If so, you've found a good one!

But now is the time to sit back and merely watch for a few days. You'll soon figure out who is respected in that particular group.

Important to know. At the other end of the spectrum lay the people who aren't respected at all.

After a few days, go ahead and answer your first question. Be succinct: do NOT drop a link in yet, even if you discuss material from your niche. Just answer that question to the best of your ability.

You'll find yourself involved in conversations after a bit of time: be very careful. Google has begun picking up LinkedIn posts. Do you really want some off-color joke you told being pulled up in search results?

You can select how often you want to hear from each group (they send a list of new topics, and old ones with new resonpses.) You'll soon get the hang of scanning until a topic that appeals to you presents itself.

Facebook

Facebook is not as casual as Twitter, nor is it as business-oriented as LinkedIn. So, what is the best way to use Facebook as part of your SEO process?

- **FB URL** (FB user-name): Once you have more than 25 fans, you're entitled to register a custom URL. Make good use of it with your primary keyword or your business name, but keep it short and memorable: good for people. Simply go to Facebook's username page and select your page from the drop-down.

TIP: Once you register your FB user-name, you're stuck with it for life! Be sure it's a good one.

You can indeed change your Page Name if you have less than 100 fans. To do so, click the "Edit Page" button at top right. Under "Basic Information", type your desired name into the "Name" field.

- "**About**" field: this one is important, but realize only 75 characters are displayed on your Wall. Make it short, SEO-friendly and sweet! Almost everyone puts their company name and a link to the site there, if under that limit. (Others use phone numbers or email addresses.)
- "**Info**" page: another good spot for keywords! Depending on the 'type' of page you registered, fields will differ here. If a field doesn't suit your company, leave it blank: it won't show up. You want links to your site, links to profiles on other SM sites (LinkedIn), your blog, and a direct link to products or services. Remember that people will be reading this info! Keep it as natural as possible, sprinkling these links in amongst your descriptive text.
- "**Updates**": keywords again! No, not the same thing repeatedly. You want variations. Can't think of any? One of my favorite sites is the Thesaurus site. Type in a word, hit enter - it provides a list of synonyms.
- **Facebook posts**: of course you'll always mention any new products, but you'll also communicate with John Q. Public there. Facebook is semi-casual in nature. Do not ever give away all your good content here. You want to give people a taste and a link: drive people to your site.
- **Photos**: Optimize them! Use those captions: include a cleverly-worded link to your site.
- "Like" box: add one of these as it's enormously important. Google DOES think well of many likes!

Twitter

The idea of Twitter is to get as many authorities following you as possible. When you tweet to an authority and get a response, all of THEIR followers see your message too: you'll see a rapid increase in your own followers. Twitter is casual. You'll respond to tweets on a certain subject: in the Twitter search box, type one of your keywords or terms, preceded by **#**. Twitter will display others discussing that 'hashtag term': respond whenever you can with help, advice, or just a joke. If you happen to enjoy a certain TV show such as Grey's Anatomy, do a search for #GreysAnatomy and you'll be instantly involved with everyone watching it with you. Here, just have fun! Respond back to anyone who responds to you: check out any new followers, and follow them in return if they're useful.

Best ways to use Twitter to increase traffic:

- **Choose a good account name.** Your business name+keyword, for instance. Oh yes, right user name too! User name appears next to your 'profile' (which, of course, you've carefully done already.)
- Hi ho, hi ho - to **SEO our Bio**... (again, couldn't resist!) 160 characters here. Make full use of every one. First, write an outline of points you'd like to make: count words. 400 words? You have chopping to do! A bio is serious: no fluff here. Cut the fluff, cut out many adjectives, and... count again. Not there yet? Evidently this is going to require major whackage. Deep breath - now delete the entire paragraph where Aunt Wanda chose your copyrighted Hoppy Ball to fly down your driveway! Does everyone really have to know that at 73, she made it whilst at 8, you wound up in the ER with a shattered coccyx bone? I didn't think so!
- Be very careful with the **first 74 characters** of that tweet you're about to set loose: the first 74 are all that are listed on Twitter pages. Your best SEO goes in those 74: burn that number into your brain! Leave the silly hashtags for the rest.

- **Killer tweets**: enter a conversation, go back and forth a bit. When you feel inspired, go for a marvelous tweet: one that grabs attention, informs, and loads of people are reading it.
- As for tweeting your own URL, **mix it up**! Not just the URL to your home/landing pages, oh no. USE your own content from other pages, then simply say "Read about (keywords) at (shortenedURL.)"
- Use Google's Shortened URL process as it retains stats for you such as how many clicked that link in which tweet.
- Whenever you tweet**, use a hashtag** or two! Just as you find interesting people by searching for certain hashtags, they locate you the same way. Don't be too fast to leap on the 'trending' bandwagon: those tweets are so numerous that yours will be off-screen in a heart-beat.
- **Connecting to Facebook from your Twitter account**: not always a good idea. Communicating in each platform is certainly different: consider how you'd feel seeing a list of current tweets on your FB page.

Use the Twitter analyis tool FollowerWonk to enhance your Twitter campaign. It's not hard -- just perform these steps:

- Sign into the tool with Twitter

- Find top followers - Followerwonk displays social authority (the higher, the better)

- Compare users - compare your social graph to that of competitors or industry leaders: you can compare users they follow or their followers. Here, you can make new connections by seeing who has high social authority, following them, and then making your own connection.

- Analyze followers - locate the most influential ones, dormant ones, geographic location of followers, social authority of those you follow, even gender and age! Counts of people you follow: how many follow them. Large numbers of followers have the most clout - you'll want to target them. This tool even shows the highest-used words in tweets!

- Track followers - see how many new or dropped off for you or a competitor

Make sure all your SM icons are on your site, blogs, and articles. Make it easy to share! People will connect with you if your content is good.

Google +

Google + has been slowly but surely steaming its way upward in importance. Now, if you are fairly well known there (make relevant posts often,) you can make one post and seconds later it appears in results on Google! That is cool, very. So. How to get the best results from Google +?

You can actually add good links to your profile: be careful with that anchor text (don't forget your keywords and/or business name,) but make the profile interesting to read as well.

Any post in Google + groups: the first sentence becomes that post's 'title tag,' which relates highly to rankings! And, unlike Twitter - here you can go back and edit posts any way you please.

A few months ago, Google announced it was allowing hashtag searches (USA and .ca to begin.) Google+ posts are shown to the right: if you're a Google+ member, you'll see responses from those you know or public ones. Moreover, getting a +1 is one of the fastest ways to get a page indexed by Google!)

Social Media Best Practices

This will truly amaze you: great content is the best practice, of course! Sure, it's a hoot to post silliness, pictures and other fun things, but. But it gets you nowhere. Post some of your own valuable content. More and more social content is becoming linkable.

How do you know what to say? I have a question for you. Who is your target audience? What type of person is interested in your topic? Once you can answer those questions, your own "What do I say" becomes simple. You communicate the way you would with a friend who's interested in that same topic, but you respond intelligently over silliness. I personally believe that one good silly tweet in the midst of a serious conversation, if well done, can put everyone on the floor and actually boost your social rank!

During these conversations, you'll be doing what's known as 'organic sharing.' This is sharing links naturally. "Funny you should mention that: I just wrote an entire piece on it you should read. I'd really be interested in your perspective. Here - www.DrivingDUI.com." That is far from "Have YOU known anyone who died because of a DUI? #DUIdeath www.DrivingDUI.com." The latter is directed to the public. People are aware of that, consider it spam - and suddenly you lose followers. Don't forget to shorten your URLs for Twitter! Typing one out can burn valuable space when character length is so very limited. I prefer goo.gl as Google hangs onto your URLs and, of course, uses them in analytics. Every time you use it, you see a list of the past URLs you pasted into it and a count of clicks it got. How handy is that!

If you don't have a Facebook account, best get one yesterday. It has very high search authority, like Google +. A great FB post with an interesting picture and good content gets around very rapidly indeed, and again pulls in yet more targeted traffic.

Social Media Do's and Don't's

You do NOT want to constantly mention your site on any social media: you'll appear "spammy" to Google, but far worse, you'll be considered an idiot. The entire idea behind social networking is to become known as an "authority" in your field, both to search engines and end-users.

Why is being an authority so much of a necessity?

When you yourself run a search for a brand new air conditioner, are you going to click on an unknown brand/outlet or a site with authority? Somewhere you trust to have real answers, not backed by a certain product.

To do for all Social Media platforms:

- If you aren't on **Facebook, Twitter, LinkedIn** or any important forums in your field, that needs to change. Use the same user name/company name for each.
- **Do not use the same password** anywhere for obvious security reasons:
- Do use passwords that are NOT your **name, your house number, anything personal** whatsoever.
- Do use an **8-9 character long password**: include a few capital letters, numbers, and @ sign.
- **Be careful about any group posting** on LinkedIn: anything you say can be popped up on a search engine. So if you're a vet talking about dogs and their behavior, you do not tell the story about how Spot farted and ruined a party!
- Definitely do for all networks: **be HELPFUL about your product or information**. If you can do so, run contests: everyone loves something free, even if it's only a mention in your 'Stars of the Month" column on Facebook! .

Chapter 5: Promote and Market your site

Do you have a really good short description for each niche site? I don't mean the META description, I do mean a short paragraph or two that accurately describes each niche's contents and does so in a manner compelling enough that anyone reading it will want to visit. Once you have a list of all 20 sites, copy it, paste it, and this time double the size of each description. Here you can add information about specific pages of interest, a list of reasons users will need to visit that site, and any other good reason that site will be popular, useful and relevant.

- This Master Site Content list will be very handy when you **join** HARO, the single best promotion tool out there and not very well known! HARO was created for reporters and tv producers who need sources. They can simply send their specific requirement to HARO (for free) and HARO will place it under the proper category (health, high tech, academic, etc.) Then the site sends out these emails twice a day to anyone who signs up for it! Again, no cost involved. You answer any of these and send your response to the email address next to that query. That reporter scans their responses. If yours fit, they contact you, often quote you and provide links to your sites as well. Killer FREE PR!
- **Hunt blogs** (not no-follow blogs) that are related to your niche. Leave RELEVANT comments with links back to your site... don't be spammy! Really read what you're responding to, and make sure your response gives good information.

- Start a **reciprocal link campaign** with other sites/blogs related to your niche. You'll trade links with them: works well for everybody.
- Again find blogs in your niche - blogs that will allow you to **provide guest posts** or story ideas. Come up with several ideas before you pitch them.
- **Press releases** - if you have a new announcement (such as a new site!) a press release is always a good idea. You can go the expensive route (www.prweb.com) or, like the rest of us, opt for the freebies. Realize that press releases are written for journalists, not the public. You're providing news.. simple as. Keep it 5 paragraphs or under, forget flowery language, do NOT put "PRESS RELEASE" in capitals at the top!
  Press Release sections:
    - **Title** (YOUR COMPANY announces/unveils/introduces/boosts...)
    - **Date** + location (if it's a site, give the URL.)
    - **Intro** (couple of lines only)
    - **Body** (facts! explain what this is about, how it happened (if interesting,) quote or two from someone in industry.
    - **Boilerplate** (your basic "about" section. Independent info on you, your company.)
    - **Contact info** (your name, address, phone.)
    - **Put ###** on the last line. Don't ask me why: it's the way press releases have ended for YEARS. You'll stick out (not in a good way) if you don't do this.
- Ensure your site looks **great on mobile devices** (we did go through that on your Wordpress theme hunt: I know you found a good responsive theme!)
- **Newletters**: if users sign up on your site, send the occasional newsletter when you update. Make sure there's a clear opt-out involved!
- **Free offer** - hugely popular. Isn't everything free a big draw? Type up an article, PDF it and offer it as a give-away. Done!
- **Contest** - Everyone loves a contest! Even when the prize is your neweseletter - free.

- **Youtube** - this is the grandfather of all great marketing tools. Make a stand-out YouTube (minus stealing anybody else's work, natch!) If this goes viral, so do your sites.
- **Marketing grader** - Hubspot's free tool that tells you what's right and wrong with your marketing.
- Remember: the very BEST marketing consists of a **damn good SEO campaign**. If you follow the steps in what you're reading, you'll have a top notch campaign. Just don't forget to check the ***site periodically: I update this book regularly with all new SEO techniques (not to mention reports on what Google is up to!)

Make sure your backlinks campaign bears fruit: this is a major marketing technique. .

Chapter 6: Free SEO Tools for Your Sites

These tools provide access to metrics you should check to ensure your SEO efforts are successful.

Google Trends

Google Trends: shows interest over time for keywords you enter. Also shows interest by geographic location: this can be enormously helpful!

Steps to check keyword interest:

- Type in desired keyword(s) at top of page, where search box says "**Explore search volumes. Type in one or more terms.**" I searched for "website design companies:"

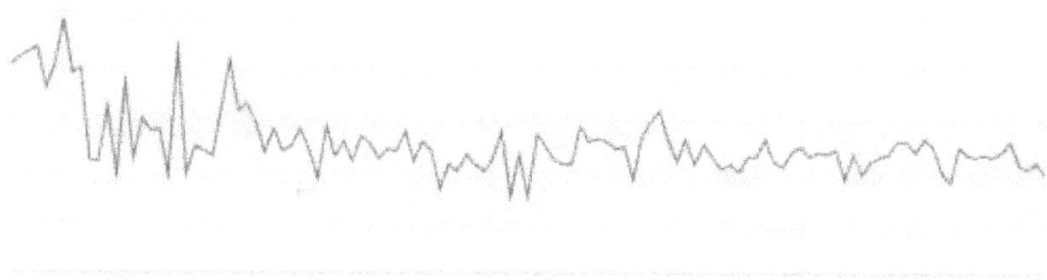

Here, you could click "**Forecast**" to see how much interest your term(s) will have in the future.

- Scroll down to see interest by region. I saw a lot of interest in India.

- Scroll down more for "**Related searches**" (related keywords, the interest for each.) This is hugely useful when you're researching terms to begin your niche sites. I see a "breakout" for "Best website design" so I clicked it, generating a new search on that term. Here, the interest is mainly in the USA! If you're an American web designer, you'd definitely consider "Best website design."

Google AdWords

Go to Google AdWords for this exercise.

Click "Tools and Analysis" on the menu, and select "Keyword Planner."

If you're returning, click "Search for keywords." Type in the one(s) you need information on, hit enter.

You can simply click "Keyword ideas" tab, and you'll see:

Ad group ideas | Keyword ideas | Download | Add all (801)

Search terms	Avg. monthly searches	Competition	Suggested bid	Ad impr. share	Add to plan
freelance writer jobs	1,600	Medium	$0.85	0%	

1 - 1 of 1 keywords

Keyword (by relevance)	Avg. monthly searches	Competition	Suggested bid	Ad impr. share	Add to plan
freelance writer job	110	Medium	$0.16	0%	
freelance writer	6,600	Medium	$2.72	0%	
freelance writers	1,900	High	$3.65	0%	
writer jobs	1,900	Medium	$0.95	0%	

Click the "Avg. monthly searches" cell and the list will re-order according to search numbers. You'll see a monstrous load of searches for "Job search": no surprise there! Competition is high, of course. Everyone and their uncle will be optimizing for "Job searches" - not at all what is needed for a niche site.

Now that you have a rough idea of search numbers, click "Keyword (by relevance)" for a sorted list with keywords closest to the one you are researching at the top. Now scroll down, keeping the number of monthly searches and competition in mind. "Writer jobs," with almost 2k searches and medium competition, looks to be a winner! Clicking the blue arrow at the end of its row will add it to your terms. For fun, click "Modify search": to the right of your current term type "+ NewTerm" and hit enter. The planner found 800 keywords: I'll want to narrow that, so I'm going to use the Keyword Planner modification menu on the left:

Targeting

All locations

English

Google

Negative keywords

Customize your search

Keyword filters

Avg. monthly searches ≥ 1,000

Suggested bid ≥ $0.00

Ad impr. share ≥ 0%

Competition: Medium

Keyword options

Show broadly related ideas

Hide keywords in my account

Hide keywords in my plan

Include/Exclude

Here, you can narrow your search by selecting a location, language(s), search engine, or 'negative keyword' (search results containing these terms won't count. It's as if they don't exist.)

You can further customize your search by:

adding "Keyword filters" (Avg. monthly search #, competition level and more,) "Keyword options," (skip for now, and "Include/Exclude" (only show keyword terms containing the terms(s) you specify here or the reverse - exclude keywords containing specified terms.) For now, type "1000" into the "Avg monthly search box" and then select "Medium" competition. Instantly the "Keyword ideas" chart will change!

First time? You'll have four possibilities:

- Search for new keyword ideas
- Get search volume for a list of keywords
- Get traffic estimates
- Multiply keywords lists for new keyword ideas

If you're researching keywords for new niches, select the top option (Search new keyword ideas.) Type in your keyword(s), skip landing page, but hit "Your product category." Click the small arrows at the far right of each category, and a new list appears. You may have to click on "Product Category" to get back out of a list: I sure did! I typed in "freelance writer jobs." No category really applied: I skipped that.

Under "**Targeting**" I started typing "En..." and "English" popped up. You can select as many languages as you like.

Under "**Keyword filters**" I played a bit: there may be a tremendous amount of info for my chosen niche! So, I edited here and there.

"**Avg. monthly searches**" >= 1000 (only show terms that have been searched for more than 1000 times over the last month)

"**Competition = medium**" -- click outside the box.

Under "**Keyword Ideas**" I could have edited and selected other locations. I didn't!

I also could have included/excluded certain terms, but I was ready for results. I clicked "**Get ideas.**"

The "Ad group ideas" screen appears as follows:

Ad group ideas | Keyword ideas | Download | Add all (6)

Ad group (by relevance)	Keywords	Avg. monthly searches	Competition	Suggested bid	Ad impr. share	Add to plan
Writer (9)	writer jobs, medical ...	45,000	Medium	$5.43	0%	
Freelance (26)	freelance writer, ho...	93,600	Medium	$1.36	0%	
Writing Jobs (7)	freelance writing jo...	33,000	Medium	$0.90	0%	
Online Jobs (7)	jobs online, online ...	60,200	Medium	$0.88	0%	
Data Entry Jobs (6)	data entry jobs from...	95,300	Medium	$0.39	0%	
Keywords like: Stud...	freelance writer jobs...	1,620,200	Medium	$0.86	0%	

1 - 6 of 6 ad groups

You could click "**Keyword ideas**": to see what happens if you do, scroll up to the previous section.

As you can see, keywords are grouped. Look at the left column for 'ad group': "writer" looks closest to what we want, as it shows "writer jobs, medical writer jobs..." Now click the ad group that most interests you, for a list of keywords, monthly searches for each one and other information. We want a good amount of searches per month! "Ghost writer" has 27k searches: far beyond any of the others. Run your cursor over the chart icon, and a chart pops up showing monthly searches (last 12.) My search could be done here... or I could continue by simply gathering a short list of good keywords.

Google Webmaster's Tool: Checking Optimisation

To check your optimization, load Google's Webmaster Tool. You'll be presented with your dashboard:

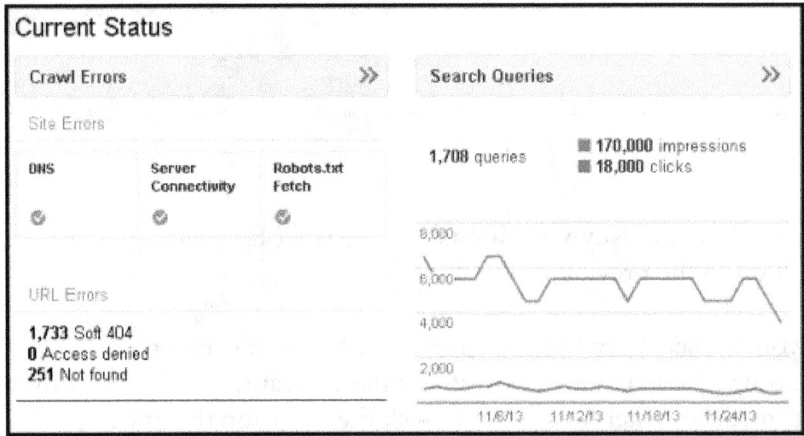

We'll start with "Search Queries", so click that now.

Each keyword shows 5 metrics, and I'll go through the most important ones you'll be tracking over time.

Impression: a keyword that has a high 'impression' number means that the particular part of your site associated with that keyword is getting some great traffic. If there's a keyword that has fallen since last month, there's part of your site that needs tweaking: new content, new description.

Clicks: they might be seeing your site in SERPs, but are they clicking? This metric will enlighten you there. CTR takes it one step further: this is the actual percentage of people clicking your site from the SERP. If this one is falling, again tweaking is needed.

See that 'With Change" button right above the chart? If you've changed your SEO strategy, click this button to see changes in these metrics over the period of time since you made changes!

Google Analytics: Checking Your Site's SEO in-Depth

Walk-Thru: Checking Keyword Success With Google Analytics

To check how successful your keywords are, sign into Google Analytics. On your menu, you'll click "Aquisitions" then "Keyword" and finally "Organic Search" as shown below.

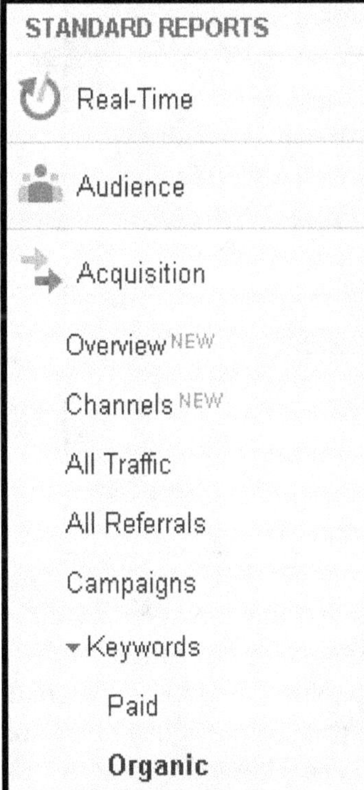

To the right, you'll see a list of keywords with various valuable metrics such as:

Visits - total # of visitors

%New Visits - percentage of total number of visitors that are new (haven't visited your site before.) If this percentage is low next to a particular keyword you've been targeting, it's time to check out another keyword for this page.

Bounce rate - if this is high for a particular keyword you're targeting, you'll need to check your content and other SEO factors: META tags, ALT tags. If this keyword accurately represents your topic and the bounce rate is high -- users are hitting this page, not finding anything they need and bailing quickly.

Organic Search Traffic

What is an 'organic' search? Good question! There are two kinds of searches: paid and organic. If you click one of the ads on Google's SERP, that is a 'paid' search. Anything else is 'organic'. Now, to drill down for particular keyword effects on traffic, click that keyword. For this exercise, pick a keyword that you did not optimize for, but had a high number of new visits. The Organic Search Traffic page appears:

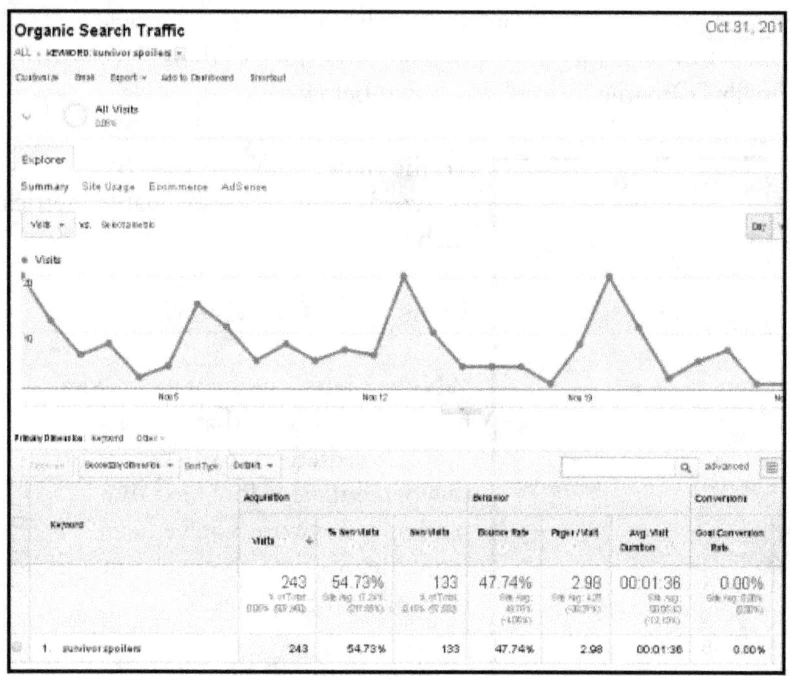

Now you'll see the exact dates when users used this term to hit your site. Now for the real fun! Say you changed your optimization (added new content to a few pages) two weeks ago. You'd like to know what effect this had on your traffic: espcially for this one keyword users are obviously interested in. You will click the "Visits" button, scroll to "Site Usage" and then select "Avg. Visit Duration" (how long the user stays on your site when they arrive.) You want to know more - how many new visitors hit during this time period?

Click "Select a new metric" and scroll to "Site Usage" and then select "% New Visits". Say you updated your content around November 8th, and the graph appears:

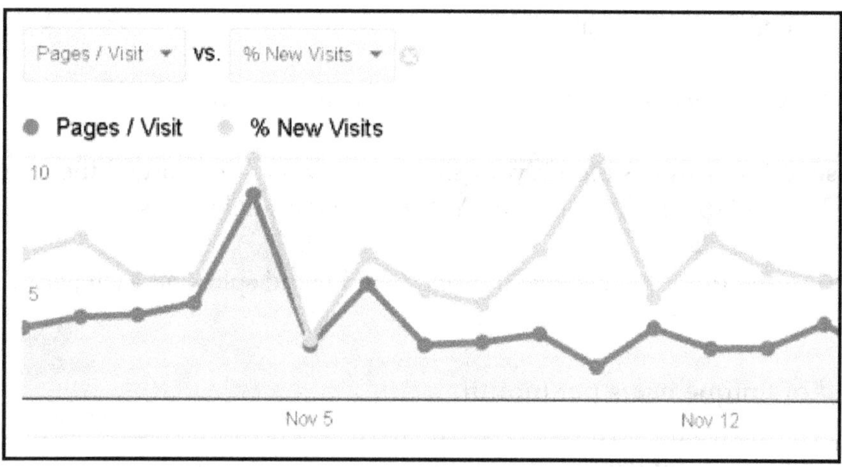

This is gold! What content did you add? Whatever it was, it blew this keyword off the map! The old content did very well around Nov. 5th: lots of good traffic who hung around and read that content plus other pages. But when you changed it.. users were still interested in the keyword, but didn't find anything of interest. That dark blue pages per visit line drops! They took one look and bailed...

You need to research your first topic. Go into depth, add graphics. Tweak that page's title and definition to include this keyword, and then check in two more weeks!

Google Analytics Various Other Metrics For Checking Traffic

Google Analytics provides so very much information that it can be overwhelming. If you follow the steps above and stick to just what is really needed to track your traffic, you're good to go. Believe me, I've spent years now delving into GA (and getting lost -- don't we all?) The following statistics are specifically what you need to know:

site referrals (how are users getting to your sites? Via Google, another site..? Referrals will tell you which spot 'referred' your site to users.) On your GA menu, once again click "Acquisitions", under it "All Referals". This is super cool! Did you wonder where users were coming from, if not an SE? Now you'll know!

direct navigation (typed-in traffic, email links, etc.)

search (terms used to hit your site from any SE -- less useful these days on Google, but Bing and Yahoo provide solid results.)

Bounce rates (percentage of users who hit and split - hit a site, click the 'back' button immediately.

# of unique users per month

# of returning users per month

If these last two numbers have dramatically decreased since last month, there is a problem. First, check Yahoo and Bing stats. Did traffic fall off on those SERPs as well? You may have an accessibility issue: people can't reach you. Otherwise, if the results are just low on Google, oops - you may have been penalized. If you just acquired the "Bible" and this Google traffic loss is recent, chances are you were nailed by Hummingbird: Chapter 10 will solve that one. If you've had the "Bible" for months, your traffic just plummeted on Google - I'd have to guess that someone hasn't been updating their Bible as they should! Likely Google has changed something else: I mention it in a Bible update which you haven't seen. I call these "GOYA" errors (nothing to do with the painter!) GOYA means, of course, Get Off Your Ass and either keep up with Bible updates or check your own SEO results more often.

Bing

Bing's Webmaster tool is very handy indeed. It doesn't have nearly the amount of data available from Google Webmaster, and that's a relief! Several very useful SEO tools:

- **SEO Reports** (on dashboard, "Reports & Data") - if there are issues on the page, they appear here. Even warns for HTML sizes over 125kb!
- **Keyword Research** tool: viewing search terms entered by users, you can actually base new content on terms that are doing well.
- **Page Traffic** - Combined from Bing and Yahoo. "Clicks from search" shows how many times links to this page were clicked. "Search Keywords" then click (View) for page's details.
- **SEO Analyzer** (Diagnostic & Tools) - Cool tool! Lists errors such as missing tags, bad title length. Click on the "Page Source" tab, and errors are high-lighted in yellow.

Yahoo

Yahoo considers the following factors when ranking sites:

- **keyword density** - no hidden search terms here! Check your density against those of your top competitors, and do so fairly often as optimal keyword densities change often.

  Try the free Ranks.NLtool to check density for a page: simply paste the URL in to their Page Analyzer Tool. (Don't forget to do the Captcha, as I do.) Not only will you see density and prominence for the optimized keywords they find (which aren't neccesarily the ones you optimised for!)
- **age** - Domain age checker is a quickie. Using the same domain as I did for the density check (http://www.mattlures.com/), I learned that the site is 10+ years old. Good to know about competition! (The SEOQuake bar also provides this info.)

- **backlinks** - I like Small SEO Tools Backlink Checker. It provides site/page rank for each backlink. Captcha again, though! Yahoo much prefers quality over quantity. Links on pages with loads of other links? Not many points there.
- **site structure** - Link Structure is a great little tool, but there are so many elements involved in correct site structure. Navigation, categories, and many more.

Of course Yahoo considers many other factors as well. It prefers primary keywords, for instance. Content is king, though. Isn't that the truth on all SE's? The major difference between Google and other SE's is the importance keywords play, now that Google hides them! Yahoo, Bing and other SE's still place a lot of weight on keyword use, which is one reason I always insist of proper keyword optimization.

Ranks.nl tools

Keyword Density & Prominence: Paste an URL into their Page Analyzer Tool for a number of very helpful results including:

Tab 1: Density & prominence for keywords the tool itself found.

Elements: this is gold! Provides the keywords used in the title, headings, and everywhere else you should be placing terms to score points. Ranks.NL gives you a little green check if it approves of your use on an element such as "bold" If not, it gives advice on how you can do better.

Links in: They use majestic SEO and SEOmoz tools for backlinks. Under Majestic SEO, click on a "links in" number and you'll be sent to majesticseo's reports.

Try the free Ranks.NLtool to check density for a page: simply paste the URL in to

Majestic SEO tools

Site explorer gives fabulous information. Type in your URL and press enter for a good report, but they prefer you to register in order to use most of their tools. Do so!

Ref. Domains: gives information on each domain with your backlink: # of backlinks, Alexa score, trust metrics.

Anchor Text - tells you what people are seeing on those backlinks.

My Traffic Has Plummeted, Help!

1. Checking Google Analytics, unique/returning user numbers have dramatically decreased since last month. There is a problem: first, check Yahoo and Bing stats. Did traffic fall off on those SERPs as well? You may have an accessibility issue: people can't reach you!

   Otherwise, if the results are just low on Google, oops - you may have been penalized. If you just acquired the "Bible" and this Google traffic loss is recent, chances are you were nailed by Hummingbird: Chapter 10 will solve that one. If you've had the "Bible" for months, your traffic just plummeted on Google - I'd have to guess that someone hasn't been updating their Bible as they should! Likely Google has changed something else: I mention it in a Bible update which you haven't seen. I call these "GOYA" errors (nothing to do with the painter!) GOYA means, of course, Get Off Your Ass and either keep up with Bible updates or check your own SEO results more often.

2. Figure out which tactics to use to enhance rank on various SEs: Google loves backlinks, Bing & Yahoo like better keywords & targeting.

3. Number of pages receiving at least one hit from SEs
    - For a niche site with 5-7 pages, all of them should be receiving traffic (due to content, meta data and so on.) You can watch trends, and when the trend rises more of your pages are appearing in SE results.
    - heck your 'not provided' figure
    - If Google reports less than 5% of your organic keyword traffic as 'not provided' (hidden as I said earlier,) you're doing well.

SEO Toolbars

There are several good SEO toolbars to consider. The MozBar is well thought of, and SEO Quake is also one of the best (a ton of metrics!) I choose the MozBar simply because it shows me exactly what I need to see, easily. And it doesn't take up your precious RAM!

SEO Tip

TIP: using these toolbars to pull up many Google results can get your IP banned! Consider using proxies, or only use the SERP results when needed.

MozBar

Install the free MozBar (toolbar for Chrome or Firefox): it checks SEO content (and much more) on your own and other sites. It displays:

- Page authority: how well a page is likely to rank on Google's search results. Moz devised this: it is very close to Google's actual Page Rank scores.
- Domain authority - measures predictive ranking strength of an entire domain.

Having rapid access to these metric is very valuable indeed: both when checking out competitors and your own SEO efforts.

MozBar also has links to many tools. My favorite is **Opensite Explorer**, which runs backlink checks.

SEOQuake bar

The free SEOQuake toolbar (Firefox, Opera and Safari) provides an enormous amount of information! It has two main features: a page overlay for SERPS and a toolbar.

The page overlay gives data for every site on the results page:

- Page rank
- # incoming links
- # indexed pages
- domain age

Better yet, you can sort on these results!

To get the most out of the overlay, on Google search click "Settings" then "Search Settings".

Turn off "Instant Predictions"

Now you can set your "results per page" to 100 instead of 25! Great for using Quake: all those results are easily viewed by simply scrolling.

On an actual page you'll see:

1. keyword density
2. link counts (external, internal, no-follow) - good for checking competitor sites too

Chapter 7: My End Results & Your Workbook

I had 20 profitable sites, two that wound up authority sites. The amount of time invested for those sites was ridiculous: where I spent nearly a year, you could be ready to go in weeks. That is why the Bible includes details even including how to find developers and writers: I want you up and generating income as soon as possible. It was vital to me, and I'm sure many of you as well.

The Bible isn't exactly small, though! How to ensure you've done the steps required for each section of site creation? Print off charts listing the steps: be religious about filling in details. Then you'll have a blueprint of how to create more sites, as well as an ongoing analysis of SEO on your sites: what you've tried, what has worked, what needs to be tweaked, and so on.

Niche SEO Workbook

This is a lot of material to remember. I sure couldn't, how could anyone else? I made charts for my own use. A bit of tweaking, and you can also use them. Of course they'd do you no good at all in a book like this one. What you need are charts that are easily read and edited. Only one way to do that: basic HTML page charts! (Most major word processors - Word, Open Office, many others) can read/edit HTML files.) To download a chart:

- Go to the page with the chart you need
- Right click and select "Save page as..."
- Find a good location for your charts, you'll save all of them there
- Open those puppies and be serious about filling them out as you go.

One last detail: where do you find these charts?

There's the rub! You acquired this book youself: these charts are specifically for you, to be used as you like. If that means providing them to friends, fine by me! Books like this one do wind up on sites where they shouldn't be, though. These charts shouldn't be available to those who acquuired the Bible illegally.

Please email me, tell me where you acquired the Bible, and I'll send you the link to these charts... you'll then also have the option of receiving Bible update newsletters. As you'll receive free Bible updates whenever SEO changes, you'll need that newsletter! No, I don't collect email addresses!

The charts will look like the following one (except with many more columns):

NICHE RESEARCH 1		
Site Name	**Products**	**Similar Sites**
redLures.com	affil: Bass Pro	4
allergicCow.com	affil: Amazon	2

Chapter 8: Advanced Techniques

HTML Primer

HTML is truly a common sense mark-up language. It consists of 'tags' which describe document content: tags enclose content as that which is opened must be closed! Sound complicated?

One of the most basic tags is the Paragraph tag. Without it, text would run together as if you forgot to hit 'enter' between paragraphs. What does the paragraph tag look like?

<p>

Now that's difficult, isn't it! Greater than sign, the 'P' for 'paragraph', and a less-than sign. But don't forget that first rule: you open it, you close it! So at the end of your paragraph you'll put:

</p>

The forward slash is the closer! So, how would a real paragraph look?

<p>Hello, world! This is my very first HTML document - from here, I'm going to continue learning until I create the first real AI computer. I predict it should take -- oh, a couple of weeks.**</p>**

ta-da! You've done it. But wait! Order today, and we'll add a bolded word! Care to guess what that tag looks like?

<b>AI computer**</b>**

If you guessed the 'b', you get a cookie. Replace the 'b' with an 'i' and presto: italics. Try a 'u' for underlining.

Brace Yourself - Creating Your First HTML!

You'll need a plain text editor such as Notepad. Open it now, and immediately save it as... what? File names are very important in SEO optimization. If you link to "RE101.html", do you think a search engine will find anything of importance that relates to your site there? Nope. As usual, a page should use a primary keyword for its name.

What would be appropriate for our first HTML file? Something that you won't forget, of course! I have just the thing... just remember, if you happen to make a fortune off this, don't forget where you found it and send 10 percent to Mason!

You are now the proud owner of GrossButPriceless.com! Gross But Priceless will sell unique, one-of-a-kind works of art created by you. Each piece is, as advertised, gross - but has a deeper meaning to certain people, ensuring that you can ask a pretty penny for what is truly a piece of... you'll soon see!

Down to business. This new page will contain your moldy bagel masterpieces, so save your file as "BacterialBagels.html". (Use no spaces, no characters except for alphanumeric ones and a dash.)

Now for the code! Simply copy and paste the following code into your file (anything green is code, whilst purple is text you yourself add):

```
<!DOCTYPE HTML PUBLIC "-//W3C//DTD HTML 4.01//EN"
"http://www.w3.org/TR/html4 /strict.dtd">
<html>
<head>
<title>Moldy Bagel Masterpieces</title>
<meta name="keywords" content="moldy bagels, mold
art, gross art, religious art, sports art">
<meta name="description" content="Gross but
Priceless presents the finest in disgusting art for
the discriminating collector.">
</head>
<body>
<h1>Bagel Masterpieces by Ima Weerdoh</h1>
<p>Ima Weerdoh has created the finest mold art
fused with religious undertones. Gross but
Priceless acquired several of her pieces after her
corpse was found as the centerpiece of her final
work of art in 2012.</p>
<p>"Mother Theresa's Bagel" was created by a unique
process that Ms. Weerdoh took with her to her
grave. All that is known is that she created a
solution comprised of cemetery dirt from a specific
grave (that of Mother Theresa for this bagel,)
dried bat's eyes, Devil's Penis seeds and other
contents she refused to divulge. The YouTube below
the photo of the bagel shows Ms. Weerhoh slicing a
bagel in half, spreading her mixture on it, then
performing a ritual during which she spun three
times whilst chanting "Mother Theresa, make
yourself shown on the winds of the earth which I
have blown!" She comes to a halt, closes her eyes
and rips an enormous fart. The camera pans down to
the bagel, covered in a whitish goop.</p>
<p>Slowly a face rises in black: it's Mother
Theresa herself.</p>
<p><img src="mother-theresa-bagel.jpg" width="491"
height="726" alt="Moldy Mother Theresa Bagel
by Ima Weerdoh" /></p>
<p>Click <a href="bagels/mother-theresa-
bagel.html">here</a> to see more bagel
artwork.</p>
</body>
</html>
```

Yahoo's Yslow Plugin - Optimize For Load Speed

Yslow is superbly userful (for anything but IE!) because it looks at your pages and suggests ways to improve their performance based on geek-related practices you certainly don't need to know! Because you'll be using Wordpress, a lot of the practices will be done for you automatically. Oh, you want to see a list of rules that Yslow goes by in order to ensure your page is faster and performs better than a rabbit in heat? Be my guest. As I said, ignore a great deal of that as Wordpress kindly does it for you. If Yslow finds code in places where it shouldn't be, code written in ways that slow down performance, or other technical issues that leave you lost - speak with your developer. Several issues that Yslow finds are easily fixed by you, however! Do you have a massive search on your front page with loads of filters? Yslow will suggest you decrease those filters. It also finds enormous graphic files: something that can be easily fixed without disturbing the physical size of the picture.

Optimze Graphic Size for Load Speed

I could rattle on about JPG compression, but I believe "making the picture smaller" works just as well! Confused? Here is an example:

I used this keyword planner ad group screen cap earlier in the book. Before any resizing, it was 45kb: that's fairly large for a screen cap as simple as this one! Beware: when you optimize graphics, you're making the picture size smaller. Common sense: if it becomes smaller, it's losing pixels: quality could decline. Normally that isn't the case: graphics meant for a screen only don't need to be high quality as your screen will only display them at a certain resolution regardless of the graphic's original resolution.

So when you play, make sure you have the original saved somehwere where it won't be touched.

Ad group ideas | Keyword ideas — Download | Add all (6)

Ad group (by relevance)	Keywords	Avg. monthly searches	Competition	Suggested bid	Ad impr. share	Add to plan
Writer (9)	writer jobs, medical ...	45,000	Medium	$5.43	0%	
Freelance (26)	freelance writer, ho...	93,600	Medium	$1.36	0%	
Writing Jobs (7)	freelance writing jo...	33,000	Medium	$0.90	0%	
Online Jobs (7)	jobs online, online ...	50,200	Medium	$0.88	0%	
Data Entry Jobs (6)	data entry jobs from...	95,300	Medium	$0.39	0%	
Keywords like: Stud...	freelance writer jobs...	1,620,200	Medium	$0.86	0%	

1 - 6 of 6 ad groups

Now for the magic (.gif, .jpg, .jpeg or .png)! We will simply make the file size smaller, not affecting the visual size of the picture at all.

Go to CompressNow. Click "Choose file", find the graphic you'd like to reduce file size. Once loaded, the "compress now" button will have the new filesize beneath it: 10.98 k in this case. Click that "compress now" button, choose a spot (and a new name) for the graphic, and presto. My new version after losing weight:

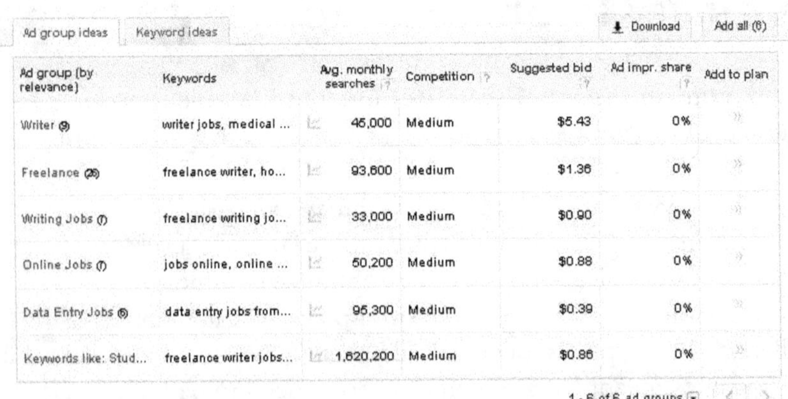

Ad group ideas | Keyword ideas — Download | Add all (6)

Ad group (by relevance)	Keywords	Avg. monthly searches	Competition	Suggested bid	Ad impr. share	Add to plan
Writer (9)	writer jobs, medical ...	45,000	Medium	$5.43	0%	
Freelance (26)	freelance writer, ho...	93,600	Medium	$1.36	0%	
Writing Jobs (7)	freelance writing jo...	33,000	Medium	$0.90	0%	
Online Jobs (7)	jobs online, online ...	50,200	Medium	$0.88	0%	
Data Entry Jobs (6)	data entry jobs from...	95,300	Medium	$0.39	0%	
Keywords like: Stud...	freelance writer jobs...	1,620,200	Medium	$0.86	0%	

1 - 6 of 6 ad groups

That is quite a weight loss: 45kb down to 11kb! Imagine if you have many larger pictures on a page, how very slow load-time would be. Run them through this converter and it's truly magic.

schema.org Article Mark-up

Want to give search engines something to really help them know exactly what your site offers, and in the process get a higher ranking, become an authority, and have SERPS display goodies such as 'author' pictures and 5 star ratings? Hint: mark-up code, used properly, will yank your ranking upward. Here's a brief example.

I googled "SEO best practices" and got the following results:

17 **SEO Best Practices** That Could Double Your E-Commerce Sales

searchengineland.com/**best-practices**-in-e-commerce-**seo**-176921
by Trond Lyngbø - in 1,218 Google+ circles
Nov 21, 2013 - These **SEO** tips have helped many e-commerce websites increase sales and revenue by large multiples, and can help you boost sales too.

Beginner's Guide to **SEO: Best Practices** – Part 1/3 - Hongkiat
www.hongkiat.com/blog/beginners-guide-to-**seo-best-practices**-part-13/
Search engine optimization is a complex subject, especially when you consider all the information and misinformation readily available online. Unfortunately ...

(That is the top of the results, by the way.) The first listing, "17 SEO Best Practices..." has something that the listing below it lacks: a tiny picture of the author. Google places a lot of trust in articles with a listed author... as you can tell because this one is literally the first result.

Welcome to mark-up code! It works with HTML, so it won't seem horribly strange. Adding it to your Wordpress theme isn't really difficult, either: you can edit your HTML by hand, or use a plug-in. There is one complex detail about mark-up code, and that is authorship. That little photo in the graphic above? Authorship code: a Google author is trusted, and has a photo to prove he is who he says he is. How to become a Google author is necessary for a lot of mark-up, so I'm going to walk you through it.

You're not a writer, you say. Why should you bother with this process? You are an authority on certain topics: when you post articles on your wp/site/blog, you do so hoping that a load of traffic will come, read, and perhaps click ads/buy products/buy services. When usersneed information available from your article, they hit Google and type in keywords (as you know very well by now!) You also know that being listed high on search results isn't a walk in the park. Google happens to put a lot of trust (and authority) into blogs with known authors. If you and 5 other people happen to post an article about the same topic, and you're a Google author? Whose article will be listed 1st? I rest my case!

Steps for Google Authorship

1. Ensure your email address has the same domain as your blog, or your WP site. This shows Google that you're legit. You'll post on that domain with the same byline as your Google + account. (If you don't have an email address for your domain, don't panic. In Step 3, Google has a work-around.)

2. In your articles, make sure the author's name is the same as your Google + name.

3. Now you're ready to link your Google + profile (picture and all!) to the content you create. You'll hit Google's "Sign up for Authorship" page, fill it in, and done.

You should also go to your Google + account and link to your content (wherever you post blogs: could be your own site or anywhere you guest-blog.) In your profile, on the right side of your "About" page, look for "adding Contributor to" links. Link to the bio on your site/blog, or link directly to the post.

Now when you guest-blog (as you should!) you'll send the correct HTML with a link to your Google + profile:

```
<a href="https://plus.google.com/1234567899999998898987?
rel=author">Your Name</a>
```

In-Depth plugin

We've all seen Google In-depth articles: if you search for a broad topic, Google will provide a section called "In-Depth". Run a search on "censorship":

In-depth articles

On Censorship
The New Yorker - May 2012
No writer ever really wants to talk about **censorship**. Writers want to talk about creation, and **censorship** is anti-creation, negative energy, uncreation, the bringing into being of ...

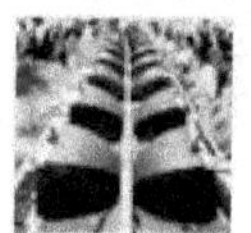

Web censorship: the net is closing in
The Guardian - Apr 2013
Eric Schmidt and Jared Cohen: Across the globe governments are monitoring and **censoring** access to the web. And if we're not careful millions more people could find the internet ...
Explore: web censorship

Google Shuts China Site in Dispute Over Censorship
The New York Times - by Miguel Helft - Mar 2010
Google said it would direct users to an uncensored version based in Hong Kong. China on Tuesday said the case would not affect ties with the U.S. "unless politicized" by others.
Explore: china censorship

Those articles come from some fairly sophisticated, famous sites. The New Yorker, The Guardian... but are only those types of articles listed in the In Depth box? Why, no.

As long as:

- your article provides high quality content to aid users in learning about a topic
- you use authorship-markup
- you have and use a brand logo (linking to your Google + page or using organizational markup)

You too can appear "in depth." For Wordpress, all you need is the Virante In Depth Articles Generator Plugin. It is simple to use, with only three fields:

- "headline" (if you leave it blank, it uses your title)
- "Alternative headline" (no need. Leave this blank.)
- "Description" short: if blank, it pulls your meta description.

That's all there is to it! The plugin generates the needed mark-up code.

Review Markup plug-in

You've seen those results with **** reviews at the top of the listing. You'd love to add a review to one of your articles, stars and all! It's simple with the Review Schema plugin.

All you do is type in the "name of the item reviewed," "URL to item," and give it a rating!

Automatically the rating is inserted at the end of your post. To move it, simply put a [rating] tag wherever you like.

General Mark-up: Boost Any Content

People write for people: microdata adds structure and content that makes sense to search engines. Engines, plural: not just Google, as Bing and Yahoo also read it. Microdata give extremely explicit information about an item, information that isn't in the visible content.

For example, you have an article titled "Ima Greatdev Presents the Most Unique Menu". Humans likely know that Ima is discussing a web menu, but a search bot may think she has a restaurant. Enter schema.org's microcode, which is simply embedded in HTML tags.

Here is part of the page as it originally appeared:

```
<h1>Ima Greatdev Presents the Most Unique Menu</h1>
<p>By Jack Green</p>
<p>Comments: 62  [the tweet icon] 245 [facebook like
icon] 420</p>
```

The same content with schema.org's code:

```
<div itemscope itemtype="http://schema.org/Article">
<span itemprop="name">Ima Greatdev Presents the Most
Unique Menu</span>
by <span itemprop="author">Jack Greene</p>
<p>Comments: 62  [the tweet icon] 245 [facebook like
icon] 420</p> **
<meta itemprop="interactionCount"
content="UserTweets:245</span>
<meta itemprop="interactionCount"
content="UserComments:>62</span>
<meta itemprop="interactionCount"
content="UserLikes:>420</span>
</div>
```

** "author" is the same as and interchangeable with HTML5's "author".

That is a very minimal example. You can also specify "audience" (intended audience for whom the piece is intended,) "award" (award won by Jack Greene for this article,) and many other properties. See the official Schema.org Article Property List for more.

Rich Snippets

What are rich snippets? A "snippet" is the description of an URL in search results. Usually Google pulls the piece of content matching whatever the user typed in (circled in red below):

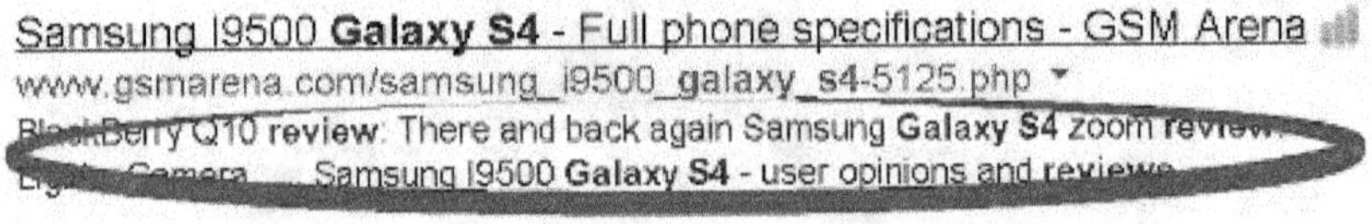

Samsung I9500 **Galaxy S4** - Full phone specifications - GSM Arena
www.gsmarena.com/samsung_i9500_galaxy_s4-5125.php
BlackBerry Q10 **review**: There and back again Samsung **Galaxy S4** zoom review ...
Samsung I9500 **Galaxy S4** - user opinions and reviews

Rich snippets are extra information about the topic such as the author, a rating (in stars,) and more. Below is a Google result of the same search (Galaxy S4 review) with rich snippets:

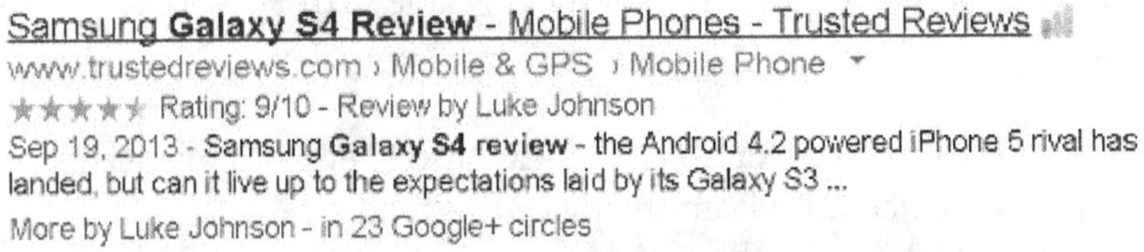

Samsung **Galaxy S4 Review** - Mobile Phones - Trusted Reviews
www.trustedreviews.com › Mobile & GPS › Mobile Phone
★★★★★ Rating: 9/10 - Review by Luke Johnson
Sep 19, 2013 - Samsung **Galaxy S4 review** - the Android 4.2 powered iPhone 5 rival has landed, but can it live up to the expectations laid by its Galaxy S3 ...
More by Luke Johnson - in 23 Google+ circles

Chapter 9: Technical Glossary

link: connection from one web resource to another: usually underlined.

Anchor text: description of where the link leads to. This is always an excellent spot to use your SEO keywords! SEs count them higher in links.

<a> The anchor element defines a link. The most important attributes:

- **href'** -- that link's destination, whether it be an URL or a named location in the same document.
  <a href="http://www.google.com">Search Google</a>

- **name** -- creates a bookmark. (notice: no anchor text needed.)
  <a name="_technical-glossary"></a>

- **mailto** -- this is a link to email.
  <a mailto="you@yahoo.com">Your name</a>

authority sites: sites that are highly trusted by Google to have content relative to the site's main topic.

Meta tags: special HTML tags that don't have anything to do with how data is displayed. Instead, they provide information about the page such as:

- a description of the contents
- the title
- a list of keywords.

Bounce rate: the percentage of users who hit a site and instantly leave.

the "fold": The invisible boundary on a web page between what the user sees, and what he must scroll down to see. "Above the fold" is the preferred spot for valuable information, as many users never bother to scroll down.

Chapter 10: Deadly JERMs for Hummingbirds

Are you familiar with the term "conversational search"? You will be soon, like it or no. Andriod certainly does: their electronic audio processing permits people to search simply by saying "search" then for what! Google knows that the ratio of mobile users to desktop/laptop is already 45%, rising to 70% in the next few years. Google is attempting to mimic Android's "conversations" right down to responses (puking out exactly what the user needs.)

Frankly it pissed me off. Losing income on one small site didn't bother me at all. The thought of other people - some of whom depend on site incomes to live - suddenly seeing their income fall badly? That really pissed me off. It also triggered my usual reaction to hearing "...and there's not a damn thing to be done about it. Keep on creating great content, using good SEO techniques as usual."

*&%!@^ **THAT**!!!

It doesn't happen often, but I went to war. Frustration mounting: papers flying as I'd pitch useless notes. Pounding on that keyboard, and then cursing the results. Loudly.

Finally the sun was rising and I was exactly where I was when I'd started: nowhere. My office certainly had gone through a few changes, though. But the question still remained unanswered. What would it take to avoid Google's barfage?

I got to a point where all I could do was kick back, stare at the screen and click the "back" button, the "forward" button. Over and over and...

There it was. If it had been any easier, it would have bit me right on the ass. As it was, with my background I should have seen it hours ago. Many hours ago.

It's more rare than tits on a bull for SEO experts to have my background: slightly less rare for tech writers. That's why it hasn't hit anyone else yet. But it will... and there will be a lot of "How did I not see that? Had grammer in high school/college/both."

If you're not a writer, you may remember some of these fun terms from English classes. I'll tell you one large secret: Google knows them well. AI me achin arse! Superlatives, adjectives, simple sentences... just a few of Google's toys you need to learn in a hot hurry.

Superlative: good, better, best. Best is your superlative: and you'd be superbly stupid to optimize for the 'best' anything, because Google got there ahead of you. Years ago, Google began putting together some of the massive amount of data they've collected: they're calling it a Knowledge Graph. This takes words, or keyword phrases, and relates them to each other. No longer will Google be looking for direct keywords: concepts will rule. Just like in conversations. Do you ever say to a friend, "best honky tonk Nashville?"

Google has put together a few concepts like that: 570 million of them, roughly. When a user happens to type in that concept, they don't just get the plain old SERP: they get the new "card". Supposedly this card has all the information necessary to address that concept. See for yourself.

Hit Google. Now type this in, word for word: "Does Barrack Obama have brothers and sisters?" Hit enter.

That, friend, is a "card". Lovely, yes? For people who own sites devoted to Obama, not so much. The user sees all that condensed information, and is on to their next search. Other SEO pros don't like that thought: for me? Red flag in front of a bull! I had a field day when first I learned about this "card" - I too realize that all that relevant information is above the fold. The rest of the results are where, then? Yup.

So, when Hummingbird becomes official, you have a new rule: "Avoid the damn card like the plague."

If you've been good about following the steps in this particular manual, you're almost there anyway: long-tail keywords are second nature to you. And that is the only real way to avoid the card! That, and knowledge of some grammer, as I said above.

Simple Sentences

Remember 'simple sentences'? They have a subject (noun) and a verb, and they express a complete thought.

"Shelley ran past."

Notice anything? That is nearly as terse as a keyword, isn't it? If I was a betting man, I'd put money on Google amassing many simple, very common sentences/questions and coming up with cards for each. A little test? Google "Compare apples to oranges" Oh! What might that be? A card.

Knowing what you do about long-tail keywords, how about changing "apples and oranges" to something a bit more specific? Add a "red" before "apple" and hit enter again. Oh! How about that... card is gone.

When Hummingbird rolls out, you'd best have that bit of info memorized.

Superlatives

You probably remember "good, better, best" as well. Been a while, maybe, but you remember it.

Good: Positive

Better: Comparative (used for two things only. "She is better than he is.")

Best: Superlative (Used for a bunch of things. "That Ferrari is truly the best.")

If you run into trouble, fill in the rest of that sentence in your mind: the best of what? Cars. All cars. How about "That Ferrari is truly the better"? No, because that sentence isn't finished, is it? "...the better of the TWO cars." Now it's finished.

Why did you just go through the pain of high school again? Because Google's little honey-sucking bird did. Whilst they love honey, they muchly prefer superlatives! Any superlative that regards well-known, major people/places/things - you'd best bet there's a card lurking around the corner. Much earlier, I showed you an example about country bars in Nashville. To carry that a bit further: you've decided that indeed one of your niches is going to be about country bars in Nashville: bluegrass pickers and all. But wait... first, you'd better test that notion.

Enter "What are the best country bars in Nashville?" NOPE. Not going to work. That superlative "best" got you. You'd be fine - if you don't mind being under that fold, if you're even on Page 1. Optimizing for superlatives: soon to be a no-no.

Now try: "what are good country bars in nashville tn?" YEP! You're in the clear... by changing one adjective!

How about "best bluegrass country bars in nashville"? NOPE We narrowed the scope but only slightly - there's that card.

Now try - "best bluegrass country bars with banjos in nashville" YEP! Your target is much, much narrower- this always works, even with a superlative. Of course it does as it's a lovely long-tail keyword.

Trending Topics

I'll leave you with one last topic to consider: anything hot, trending, heard on the Late Show every night. Here's a typical one:

Type in "What is gluten?"

Google loves that one! Gluten is on everyone's tongues (and it makes stuff taste like crap, I might add.) However, to Google it tastes like that proverbial honey. Look at the sheer size of that card!

One day you're ill: you go to the doc, and you hear that you too are now on board. You are into the gluten craze yourself! Might as well create a niche for it. You trot to the grocery and buy a bunch of 'gluten-free' products... but back at home, you're stumped. An idea occurs, but surely not... you type in "gluten allergy" and... YES! (Not that you'll use this: you used LongTailPro and found the competition stratospheric.)

If you discover that one of your topics has a card, read the dang thing. Avoid optimizing for the (usually general) information in that card.

Is This the End of the Bible? No...

As I just discussed, changes are on the horizon. For SEO people, changes are always either in the "oh hell it's today" or "word has it that within the next year..." Whichever way it happens, your techniques must evolve as the search engines are evolving. It's all aimed at a 'better user experience': that's what we all intend to do. Provide knowledge, entertainment, services -- and make a buck or two in the process.

I believe we're currently in the midst of what I'm calling a Webolution. It's been sneaking up: smart phones growing like weeds, for instance. Voip is struggling to keep up: Android has made several large steps in that direction. My S4? I can go for days without touching it. It tells me I have a text, and from whom. I say "reply" and blurt an answer, never missing one stroke typing.

Of much more significance, I say "Search"... It certainly isn't ready for prime time yet, even the Android voice technology. But with APIs such as webRTC (sounds geek, but it simply means a new way to put audio and or video simply into a browser. The browser gets this technology: minus plug-ins, extensions, codecs, stand-alone apps... you click to open a page and voila. You're talking to your friend in Boomphock, Alaska.)

Skype, you protest. No more Skype! Your Firefox or Chrome or Safari (NOT your IE lol) will allow direct, real-time communication with no lag.

Google is merely staying ahead of the curve, as they always have. Me? I'm right behind them: sometimes neck and neck. You? You're right behind me, because just like SEO, this book doesn't end here.

I'll be updating it whenever change is in the air. You simply need to hit Freelance SEO Services, sign up for the Bible Newsletter, and it will send you an alert each time this manual is updated.

That newsletter might just do another thing or two: all in good time!

Speaking of good time, I certainly hope you both enjoyed and learned from this manual! SEO isn't intensely high-tech, nor is it witchcraft. It's simply checking stats, tweaking here and there. That's it! The fun comes in knowing what to check and how to change: ergo this manual. There simply isn't another one like it. God knows I know that - I searched until my fingers fell off.

As they're liable to do any moment now.

-- **James L Mason**, ***Ultimate SEO Bible*** : 12/22/2013

www.ingramcontent.com/pod-product-compliance
Lightning Source LLC
Chambersburg PA
CBHW060942050326
40689CB00012B/2544

* 9 7 8 1 4 9 4 8 3 4 4 0 1 *